THE LINGUA FRANCA OF THE CORPORATE BANKER

Copyright © Julia Streets 2012

The author reserves the right to object to derogatory treatment of the work. The author has asserted her moral right to be identified as the author of this book in accordance with Section 77 of the Copyright, Designs and Patents Act 1988.

All rights reserved under international and pan-American copyright conventions.

The contents of this publication, either in whole or in part, may not be reproduced, stored in a data retrieval system or transmitted in any form or by any means, electronic, mechanical, photocopying, recording or otherwise without the written permission of the copyright owner and publishers. Action will be taken against companies or individual persons who ignore this warning. The information set forth herein has been obtained from sources which we believe to be reliable, but is not guaranteed. The publication is provided with the understanding that the author and publisher shall have no liability for errors, inaccuracies or omissions of this publication and, by this publication, the author and publisher are not engaged in rendering consulting advice or other professional advice to the recipient with regard to any specific matter. In the event that consulting or other expert assistance is required with regard to any specific matter, the services of qualified professionals should be sought.

Published under licence 2012 by Searching Finance Ltd.

ISBN: 978-1-907720-58-1

Typeset and designed by Deirdré Gyenes

THE
LINGUA FRANCA
OF THE
CORPORATE BANKER

AN EXPLORATION
AND EXPLANATION OF THE
*IDIOM*SYNCRASIES
OF BUSINESS

(glossary of more than 500 expressions included)

By Julia Streets

About the author

JULIA STREETS is best described as an odd mix of marketeer, entrepreneur and comedienne.

By day Julia runs Streets Consulting, her business development, marketing and communications consultancy. Her firm helps a fast-growing list of domestic and international financial services and technology firms explain to their customers, prospective customers and the industry at large, why and how they can make their working lives better.

Julia started out working for Price Waterhouse (now Price Waterhouse Coopers), cutting her business teeth at a global PR firm (Hill and Knowlton, part of WPP Group), rising through the ranks at Instinet, (global agency brokerage firm), before being headhunted as Global Head of Communications for the technology business of the global stock exchange, NYSE Euronext.

In her spare time Julia is a stand up comic, compere, after-dinner speaker and singer/songwriter and has been featured on BBC Radio 4's Today Programme, BBC Radio Kent and in the City media. In 2011, Julia was invited to join the Board of Trustees of the charity, 'Children in Crisis' which seeks to educate children in some of the most remote parts of the world and in 2012 was selected to become a Fellow of the British American Project.

About Searching Finance

For more information, please visit www.searchingfinance.com.

CONTENTS

Acknowledgements vii

Buzzword bingo xi

PART 1 THE WORLD OF CORPORATE LINGO 1

Introduction 3

Chapter 1 The target for the key learnings from this brain dump 5

Chapter 2 Careering words 7
Left of field from across the pond 7
'Corporate bankers' 8
Climbing the greasy pole 11
Demystification and simplification 14
Why make anything more complicated than it need be? ... 15
Flying solo 16
People do business with people they like 18

Chapter 3 Why do we do it? 21
Young, blinding and cutting edge? 22
Innovation breeds jargon 24
Language tribes 26
It's not all about knowing it all 28
Present, presentable and presence 29
Speaking their language 30

Chapter 4 I am not alone 33
The top 10 office irritations 33
Top ranking irritating jargon 34

Economic with invention 38
When it feels like you can't go on 42
Opening the kimono on your sweet spot? 43
Drinking the Kool Aid 44

Chapter 5 Bullshit Bingo **47**
Grid to play your own game of bullshit bingo (pen not included) .. 53

PART 2 GLOSSARY OF EXPRESSIONS **55**

Glossary of expressions **57**

Appendix – A selection of baseball expressions **133**

Endnote: Please do get in touch 137

ACKNOWLEDGEMENTS

My thanks to everyone who has inspired and encouraged me in every aspect of my mixed up, rather odd life. It is rare to be given the opportunity to publicly thank my friends and family. I am blessed with loving and faithful support from them, their advice and their company, which I greatly treasure.

When Ashwin Rattan at Searching Finance approached me before a gig in December 2011, without even having heard a line of my comedy, he offered to publish anything I would care to write (I imagine within reason, but generously he didn't give that impression). It was quite a leap of faith on his part and I hope this book does him proud alongside his other highly-qualified and accomplished authors.

I am surrounded by an amazing team of talented professionals at Streets Consulting, not least the ever-supportive Sybille Mueller. Without them, none of these words would ever have met paper and I am hugely grateful for all their hard work and dedication. Additional thanks to Marlon Duncanson for designing the cover, Eamonn McCormack for his patience in taking the cover photograph and Lindsay Clarke for proof reading this weird collection of thoughts.

I hope they know this because I do tell them, but thank you to all our clients who entrust their brands to Streets Consulting and to you I promise that no clients have been harmed in the making of this book. To my network of business and personal contacts, especially those who responded to my requests for assistance with this book, thank you for your support and I hope you find your reference.

THE LINGUA FRANCA OF THE CORPORATE BANKER

Thank you for buying my book – unless it is a gift, in which case I thank the giver and applaud them for their discerning taste. I hope it serves to be practical and you enjoy reading it as much as I have enjoyed writing it.

To my nieces and nephews.
I hope to inspire and encourage,
as others have done for me.

Buzzword Bingo

Buzzword bingo
What a lot of jingo
Learn the lingo you'll go far
If you nail it's never going to fail
It really helps you raise the bar

Expressions we are haemorrhaging
Like liaising and leveraging
Ball parks and touching base
Out of boxes we are thinking
As we're nudging and a-winking
Let's cut to the chase

Buzzword scrabble
What a lot of babble
Have a dabble, have a grope
It's not rocket science, strategic alliance
Really push your envelope

From hymn sheets we are singing
Instant messages we're pinging
Really trying to buck the trend
We never tire, we're never flagging
From the value we are adding
Rules are made to bend

Buzzword snap
Draw a mind map
Analyse the GAP and SWOT
Critical acclaim
Er, it's a no brainer
Give it all that you've got

THE LINGUA FRANCA OF THE CORPORATE BANKER

The edges, they are leading
They're cutting and we're bleeding
The wheel we never reinvent
To win we're being daring
And the circles we are squaring
For out of shape we're never bent

Keep your eyes on the prize
See if it flies
Ducks in a row
Win-win scenario
The eggs that we are breaking
For the cakes we're over-egging
Get critically aligned
And shift your paradigm
We need a step change
Not a zero sum game
The message is clear,
The bang for your buck … stops here

Buzzword bingo
What a lot of jingo
Learn the lingo you'll go far
If you nail it's never going to fail
It really helps you raise the bar

Be a mat nor a mouse
When you shout 'House!'
What're you trying to really say?
When you use the lingua franca
You become a corporate wanker
It's just sweet FA

Lyrics from one of the songs in *'Streets in the City'*
© **Julia Streets, 2009**

PART 1
THE WORLD OF CORPORATE LINGO

INTRODUCTION

LIKE SO MANY things in my life, this book started unintentionally and the offer to write it came completely *out of the blue*.

In this highly competitive world of *dog-eat-dog*, firms need to explain clearly who they are, what they do, who they do it for, how they help the people who buy their products or services and explain why and how they differ from anyone else in the market. This is what I – and my talented colleagues at Streets Consulting – endeavour to advise clients day in, day out.

That's the day job, which apparently I am very good at because people tell me I shouldn't give it up. In my spare time I try to be a stand-up comic, after-dinner speaker and am a member of *Funny Women*, the network of female comedians. Over the years, I have developed material which I perform in different forms ranging from a full hour-long show called '*Streets in the City*', which I have performed at the Edinburgh Fringe Festival and other regional festivals, to shorter sets and vignettes adapted for different occasions. I continue to develop new material and my grand plan for 2012 was to write a new show. In December 2011, I performed at the Financial Services Club at the Institute of Directors in the City where Ashwin Rattan, publisher at Searching Finance, approached me and asked whether I would like to write a book. Who could refuse the opportunity, and the new show has been put to one side while I have focused on 'The Lingua Franca of the Corporate Banker'.

'The Lingua Franca of the Corporate Banker' is designed to offer a seriously light-hearted view on corporate language, how it is regularly abused, used to confuse and why I would choose to ban it. Business is riddled with it and many ridicule it, giving me the privileged opportunity to lambast and lampoon it. I do not seek to be too judgemental or school ma'am-ish in my style, it certainly is not a lesson in grammar or sentence construction. Rather, I would hope to make a case for using clear and simple language in our communications, to explore why I got sucked into using buzzwords and why others too have fallen – and continue to fall – into similar traps.

I am not alone. Over the past six months I have been casually dropping into conversation my intention to write this book. People have told me of their frustration and irritation, how they privately laugh at colleagues who use corporate jargon and the endless hilarity that management emails provide as employees unpick what they really mean.[1] As part of the research phase, I emailed hundreds of business and personal contacts from around the world to seek their opinions and have included many of the responses. I call it research, others call this 'crowdsourcing'. My thanks to everyone who replied for their responses, anecdotes and also encouragement to write this book. From the sentiment of the responses, it seems I carry something of a burden of responsibility to vent the frustration of so many.

---

1 E.g. I am sure they do love their family but did they really give up an annual salary, car allowance, gym membership and pension contributions to spend more time with them?

CHAPTER 1
THE TARGET FOR THE KEY LEARNINGS FROM THIS BRAIN DUMP

"I'm not just a PR person, I'm a PRtist. I'll create a campaign which will set your world on fire, which technically makes me a PRrsonist." Extract from show *'Streets in the City'*

THIS BOOK is written with two intentions.

It is a chance both to ridicule and remind readers that when we're not *thinking outside the box* and *going gangbusters for paradigm shifting solutions*[2], there is a serious point about the value of clear and easy to understand communication, not least given that we work in a global and highly competitive market.

My fear is that younger entrepreneurs and business people with aspirations of leadership positions run the risk of absorbing and losing themselves in language which they believe will make them sound smarter, but won't.

"I want to insert an electrode in my boss's head and every time he *manages my expectations* I want to press a button and send an electrical current to his brain. It drives me mad." Professional development coach

The international workforce which wants to trade with the UK, or which offers specialist skills and services that contribute

---
2   Italicised references can be found in the glossary of terms.

to the success of UK businesses needs to be able to understand what in this big, wide commercial world we are are talking about.

As well as hinder, I hope it will help.

The second part of the book offers a glossary. It includes some of the many, many expressions we use every day in business. Some are buzzwords, others simply expressions and idioms sprinkled throughout the working day. When I first started, my goal was to collect approximately 200 and I was sceptical that this would be possible. I tried to stop when I tipped over the 500 threshold and I still receive emails citing expressions both new and old. My hope is the glossary of terms will be useful to many international professionals, particularly those for whom English is not their first language.

It must be hard enough to trade in a language which is not your own, but *getting your noodle around* references to *soup to nuts* projects and *drinking the Kool Aid* must be confusing.

For those of us guilty of using these expressions, I hope this will serve to amuse and remind us all that *at the end of the day*, when *taking a deep dive* and *dedicating some headspace* to the *state of play* on a *drains up approach,* can we please pause for breath and explain clearly what we really mean.

CHAPTER 2
CAREERING WORDS

MY FIRST JOB was in 1989 at a global accountancy firm, then called Price Waterhouse, or as many people called it 'PW' (for best effect, read aloud in a mid-Atlantic-twang-of-an-accent). Not as an accountant, but as a secretary. Having achieved less than adequate A-level grades, further education was not on the cards. I had to consider a different career path and enrolled on a diploma course to learn how to become a professional personal assistant. Armed with lightening shorthand and typing speeds, my fellow students and I each embarked on a compulsory week of work experience. I was to spend my week at the accountancy firm working on the 24th floor of the exotically named 'Southwark Towers', today the location of 'The Shard' skyscraper by London Bridge station. As I handed in my temporary pass at the end of the week, I was handed a job offer for £9,225 per annum (to my mind a small fortune at the time) to work for a dozen newly-qualified accountants. This marked my first business encounter with young ambitious executives, all bright-eyed (despite working insanely long hours) and keen to make their mark, as was I.

Left of field from across the pond

One of my bosses was a young American and I was instantly intrigued – and became slightly obsessed – by her use of weird and wonderful expressions. She had *issues* coming at her *left of field* which were *beyond the ballpark* and man, could she *slam dunk*. One stuck with me, which I have never heard since. She referred to an associate[3] as a '*bump on a log*'. I was clueless, but could only presume that it wasn't complimentary. Only today have I looked it up to realise that I have completely misunderstood its meaning. I thought '*bump on a log*' means that someone is rather rough around the edges, ugly even. I am wrong. Today nearly a quarter of a century later, I have finally discovered that:

> "If someone sits or stands somewhere like a bump on a log, they do not react in a useful or helpful way to the activities happening around them. Don't just sit there like a bump on a log, come and help us!"

And I thank the Cambridge Idioms Dictionary, 2nd ed., for enlightening me.

Not content with one source, I had to double-check. The McGraw-Hill Dictionary of American Idioms and Phrasal[4] Verbs offers a useful example, somewhat sullied, I am afraid, by the choice of name.

> "like a bump on a log
>
> Fig. completely inert. (Derogatory.)
>
> Don't just sit there like a bump on a log; give me a hand! You can never tell what Julia thinks of something; she just stands there like a bump on a log."

'Corporate bankers'

Within a year or two, I had been promoted to work for a partner at the firm. He was – and can only imagine he still is – the

---

[3] I recall wondering what was wrong with 'colleague', however 'associate' felt very respectful. Has since been downgraded to 'co-worker'.

[4] Yes, Phrasal.

epitome of the 'corporate banker'. He would refer to me as his 'secreeeetary', refer to hangovers as 'overhangs' and put out 'best guestimates' all delivered with a sideways glance to check that I indeed did 'see what I did there, clever eh?', followed by a wink. Yes, he was a winker.

He genuinely believed that he was the smartest person on the planet, which is fair enough; however, he would take great effort and delight in making other people look and feel small and inadequate to exaggerate his supposed greatness. Over the years, I have observed that executives who do this ultimately achieve the opposite. It is a sure-fire way to undermine any respect they might actually deserve. Some of the most successful and incredibly smart executives I have had the pleasure of working with – some of whom truly are rocket scientists – possess the grace to make everyone around them feel worthy, not worthless. They would inspire and encourage, not conspire to undermine.

One paragraph is more than enough to spend on that boss, and for the one of him, there have been many, many others who have inspired, encouraged and actively supported my career path which has led me to running my business today. That 'winker's' only value to this book (other than a moment of cathartic remembrance) is to assist in explaining the title, in particular the reference to 'corporate banker' for the benefit of any international readers.

The use of 'banker' is not to suggest this book is about financial services and banking. You may have heard of cockney rhyming slang? Cockney rhyming slang is a vernacular of its own, worth being aware of when you do find yourself in London. If I mention my 'blood and blister' I am referring to my sister. Your 'boat race' is your face and to make a call you must pick up the 'dog and bone', telephone. Cockney rhyming slang is the language of the 'Cockneys', most famously represented by the Pearly Kings and Queens of East London. Traditionally, a Cockney is born within hearing distance of the

Bells of St Mary-le-Bow Church, and today the term is used as a more generic description of someone from the East End of London. Should you find yourself in the financial services district known as the City, or the Square Mile, St Mary-le-Bow Church is found on Cheapside near Bank Tube station and well worth a visit.

In keeping with and as a natural evolution of Cockney rhyming slang, it is not uncommon that words which are best not used in polite company are are substituted with rhyming replacements. When I refer to a 'banker' I mean a 'wanker'. I will let you look this up elsewhere. I have not included it in the glossary and it would be wrong of me to encourage it. (That said, it is a word which is extremely satisfying to express and should never been erased from the English language. Just choose your company wisely.) I do not seek to bash bankers, as seems to be a popular sport these days. I tried unsuccessfully to find a popular rhyming word. Lingua franca of the corporate tanker, anchor, hanker, rancour....none work as well as banker and when I tested the title with people known and unknown to me, 'The Lingua Franca of the Corporate Banker' always raised a smile, and so it stuck.

In writing this book, it seemed to flow fairly easily yet time and again I grappled whether or not to use two words: bullshit and banker. The song at the front of the book is actually entitled 'Bullshit Bingo' named after the game to which I refer in a later chapter. As you will also learn (as have I over the course of writing this book), it transpires I am something of a prude. I have decided to spare the blushes of readers to change many of the references from 'bullshit' to 'buzzword'. Interestingly when I suggested to friend that I planned to do this, her reaction was most insistent 'but all this slang is bullshit! You shouldn't change it because you'll undermine the frustration'. For this reason, some instances have remained.

Climbing the greasy pole

My fascination with corporate language and the adoption of new idioms and expressions accelerated in the early 1990s when I entered the heady world of international public relations. Realising I was never going to progress my career in the world of accountancy and increasingly irritated by my boss, I left to join the global PR firm, Hill & Knowlton, first to work in the chief executive's office and soon to become PA to the deputy chairman, under whose tutelage I grew and developed into a young executive.

As I was forging my career, Jennifer Saunders' successful TV show 'Absolutely Fabulous' ruled our screens featuring a wildly unbelievable – yet to those in the industry, entirely credible – consumer PR advisor, Edwina Monsoon. Overnight, like her, we called everyone 'Sweetie Dahling', simply because we too had 'PR Consultant' emblazoned on our business cards.

As young consultants peering out from our glass ashtray offices at the big smoke of the City beyond, we created campaigns we believed would change the world. Hill & Knowlton was and still is one of the world's largest 'full service' agencies, meaning there were many different divisions filled with young idealists specialising in a range of sectors. I worked in financial services, where I spent my day earning my pinstripes immersed in all matters financial. There were other much sexier divisions in the firm. The food group was populated with 'execs' who seemed never to stop eating; in the sports and marketing division they seemed never to sit still. I determined that the healthcare division must have been the hardest divisions in which to work when I found a girl on the kitchen floor in tears. When I asked her what was wrong she sobbed: "I'm working on a depression drug and it's really getting me down". One responsibility of the healthcare's departmental PA was to answer the phone for her colleagues. The poor girl battled with hayfever which seemed particularly to strike when she lifted the 'dog and bone'. I shudder to imagine what a caller would have thought when she answered the phone "Achtoo! Achtoo! Achtoo! Hello Healthcare"?

It seemed to me that at the time the perception of the PR industry was changing, not helped by the 'AbFab' mentality that all PR professionals were 'fun'amentalists schweettie'. (I don't know for sure that this expression was actually used in the show, but it seems very fitting.) In the corporate and financial world we were fighting to be heard and to be taken seriously. One impact of the TV show was that despite our earnest efforts, we were increasingly being viewed as the 'fluffy' PR people. Despite our campaigns making measurable impact on sales and business growth for our clients, the management consultants were stealing the limelight as the serious business gurus and claiming the prize of the valued and *trusted advisor*. We wanted to be taken just as seriously.

I recall in my mid-twenties sitting in a wine bar with other – I almost want to say thrusting but you'll appreciate my hesitation – young professionals. Between sophisticated sips of most likely the cheapest white on the wine list, we wondered how we could make our corporate clients take us more seriously. How could we become more 'highbrow', carry more 'gravitas' and bring more 'grey hair' to the table? (The last a colossal oxymoron when you are barely out of school and scraping together the train fare to work.)

We quaffed, debated and concluded that in an effort to be at least compared with the management consultants, we should *play them at their own game* and speak their language. If they could *touch base*, so could we. There was nothing to prevent us from *kicking off vis-à-vis facilitating a brainstorm* to run some *ideas up the flagpole to see if they would fly*, without *overegging any cakes* – obviously – and then *circle back*. Our *goal posts could be moved* too, goddammit.

And so began my foray into business buzzwords. I bandied expressions like they were going out of fashion. I *reached higher, added value* and *moved upstream* like never before. Expressions oozed from my every pore and I *networked, socialised* and *PR'd-it* like I was competing in an Olympic sport. I bamboozled, blinded and veritably glazed my non-PR friends with my linguistic diatribes as, wide-eyed, they exchanged glances between them, clueless with couldn't-care less.

And then, my *paradigm shifted* on a global axis.

Fast forward a decade and I was head-hunted by a US-headquartered global brokerage firm, Instinet. I went in as humble PR girl, slightly terrified by the mystique of the trading floor. I tiptoed around rows of 'sales traders' who jabbered into telephones called 'turrets' and clicked brightly-coloured keyboards, furiously tapping orders into software 'platforms' which filled their screens with graphs, charts and news updates.

What on earth did these people do all day?

It was there I quickly learned an important lesson. If I couldn't understand what they did at their trading desks and why it mattered, how could I possibly hope to explain it to anyone else or convince them that the firm I worked for did it better than any other? So I set out to quiz and question everyone I met about what they did all day. If I didn't understand the jargon, I'd ask again and again (I must have been very irritating) and then I tried to explain it in my own words to other people. If others seemed confused, it was probably me and the way I was explaining it, so I'd adapt by finding other examples and using other expressions. I would like to think that I was doing something right because within a few years, I was promoted to run the European marketing and communications department. One of the early decisions I made was to physically move the department onto the trading floor. Like so many marketing and communications departments, we were tucked away in offices at the end of corridors no-one passed along, which neither helped us understand the business nor helped the business understand how the marketing and communications function could help them. We needed to work more closely, because the stakes were getting higher.

More regulation was a-coming and coming fast. Of one thing the financial services industry can be always sure – increasing regulation. In the early half of the new millennium, a driving wind of regulatory change was blowing across Europe. In an effort to create a harmonised single European financial market, Brussels was pulling together directive after directive designed to provide a common structure. Closer to home, Paul Myners, now Lord Myners, published a report entitled 'A review of institutional investment'. For the first time Lord Myners revealed, explained and examined the roles, responsibilities and requirements of every participant in the investment process, from pension fund trustees, fund managers, consultants, research analysts, trading desks and the brokerage relationship.

Demystification and simplification

In times such as these, it is important that the regulators, industry associations and media fully and clearly understand what you do, where you fit, how you charge and how you improve the performance of your customers in the investment chain and – ultimately – the end investors. So the first approach we took with all the marketing was to simplify and demystify the language so that everyone could clearly understand what it meant and the benefits on offer. I cannot deny that there were likely instances where we *utilised, facilitated,* and *globalised the proposition,* and I can be sure that there would have been some trading and technology jargon, but where possible we pared this back in the hope that people might understand what we did for a living and why it mattered.

When I took over the department, my predecessor left a legacy of *liaising* and *leveraging*. In every meeting, the team would talk about *liaising* with John or Jane about something. To their credit they could at least spell it, but it drove me mad.

Talk to John. Speak to Jane. Who knows, you might even be able to work with them or help them. You should only leverage if you are a physicist and use levers and pulleys. (If we leverage, why don't we pulley?) Besides to my mind the only person who should be allowed to use leverage is the global head of purchasing of Unilever, as truly they do have Unileverage. We did neither, and I banned the use of both words.

Why make anything more complicated than it need be?

My roles at the brokerage firm extended quickly and broadly. Not long after having been promoted to head of marketing and communications for Europe, I was given additional responsibility for 'sales development' and later a commercial business line to sell 'independent research'.

Daily I worked with colleagues from across Europe and it was essential that they were engaged and understood every step of the sales and marketing process. This is not to suggest that they were not linguistically brilliant. I was regularly humbled by their talents and impressed by their ability to successfully conduct business in a language not their own. But why, in a highly competitive world, make anything more complicated than it need be?

Every Monday morning I would chair a European sales conference call designed to review the progress of the sales campaign, provide information updates and ensure everyone had all they needed to do their jobs and achieve their targets.

As a matter of course, I would offer further explanation if – and mostly not – required. Too often to disregard, I would be told that the individuals had understood the main elements of the call but asked what was meant by some bizarre English expressions. I forget all of them and wish I had written down, but I am convinced that they included 'pushing the envelope'.

> "Pushing the envelope confused me. I thought the person I was talking to was offering me a bribe."
> Romanian Communications Executive

The point stuck.

I become very annoyed to witness English people speaking too quickly or still raising their voices at foreigners, rolling their eyes frustrated at having to explain a concept or thought more than once. If we cannot be bothered to learn any other language to a standard with which we can communicate in business or in any other context, let us at least have the decency and courtesy of speaking clearly, at a sensible pace, leaving out confusing idioms and expressions.

This lesson also applied during my brief tenure working for the Atos Euronext, the technology business of the stock exchange NYSE Euronext. I spent two days per week in Paris and found myself on a long-haul flight every few weeks. The importance of clear communication continued to instil itself as an important discipline for global business.

Flying solo

In my mid-thirties I set up my own business. I had left the stock exchange and decided to take some time out to recover from a demanding role. This was when I first turned my hand to stand-up comedy. Throughout my career too many people to ignore have suggested I give it a go, and I had a burning feeling that if I did not take this opportunity I would always regret not having tried. Working under the direction of the talented and ever-patient Sioned Jones, I presented my first foray at The Edinburgh Fringe Festival to mixed reviews about the steadiness and consistency of my performance. I am not making excuses[5], however it is worth noting that one week before travelling to Edinburgh I had a conversation with my doctor which went something like this:

---
5   which means that I am actually making excuses.

Doctor: so Julia, to assist with your continual dizziness which might well be a case of labyrinthitis, given that it is confining you to lying still in a darkened room, it is really important that you have complete rest and avoid any stressful situations over the next few weeks. Do you have a relaxing summer planned?

I returned from the Edinburgh Fringe at the end of August exhausted yet excited by what I had learned and was determined to develop and improve both my material and my performance. But this would have to wait. My bank account was drained, as would have been the sense of humour of my bank manager before long. I needed to find a job, and quickly. The very day I decided to call a recruitment firm and put myself back on the job market, a call came in from Instinet about a freelance job to help them promote a new business.

The assignment was to help launch a new type of stock exchange. In November 2007, the European Commission issued a directive called the Markets in Financial Instruments Directive, better known as MiFID, the fruits of years of Eurocratic labour in figuring out how to create some pan-European consistency (as I mentioned earlier). MiFID brought into effect a number of fundamental changes, the most significant being to remove the so-called 'concentration rules' which had dictated that if an investor wanted to buy or sell a stock, it had to be traded on the national stock exchange. For the first time, the regulators introduced competition, paving the way for a new breed of pan-European stock exchange called a 'multilateral trading facility' (itself, a rather complicated way of describing an exchange). Chi-X Europe was the first to launch, and working with the founding executives, my job was to tell the world about it. When it was launched, this new exchange was ten times cheaper, used technology which meant you could place your orders, receive your confirmation messages and send any cancellation instructions on average ten times faster than if you traded on the other exchanges region by region. Trading participants could markedly reduce their costs and improve their trading performance, all of which matters for the end investors – you, me, and specifically, our pension and investment funds.

A really important consideration in promoting this business was to use clear, easy to understand language to explain how this pan-European stock exchange would benefit investors both in the UK, Europe and across the world. When you are dealing – pun intended – with traders who are under pressure day in and day out, you have to talk their language: get right to the point, right now, or they might cut you off with a sentence likely ending in the word 'off'. Journalists needed to be able to understand how the exchange worked and what it offered, and it was my job to explain it as clearly as I and the business possibly could. Chi-X Europe was Streets Consulting's first client and we are proud to continue to represent the exchange today.[6]

People do business with people they like

Business leadership experts talk about the power of communication, the power of leadership, the power of charisma in business. A piece of sales advice I was taught during my days at Instinet has never left me: 'people do business with people they like'. True, your product or service needs to help your clients and prospects. True, your product or service needs to work and deliver what it promises. And true, it has to be priced correctly. But we live in highly competitive times and if you can make yourself more likable by not wrapping everything up in unnecessary corporate or technical jargon, all the better. I would even argue that if you use such language, you may even

---

6   Chi-X Europe was launched in March 2007 and bought by BATS Global Markets in November 2011. Today the business is called BATS Chi-X Europe and in July 2012 reported an average pan-European market share of 24.6%. Nearly one quarter of the value of shares traded in Europe does not get traded on the traditional stock exchanges, it gets traded on BATS Chi-X Europe, the largest pan-European stock exchange by market share.

appear elitist and 'clubby', which may put people off and keep customers at bay.

Television programmes tell us we need to 'declutter' our homes and simplify our lives to give us some clarity. I would argue that we need to declutter our language. After all, isn't it so refreshing to have a straightforward conversation with someone who knows what they are talking about, to be able to understand what they mean and how it affects you? We don't do it at home. We don't give our children *guestimates* or take a *drains up* approach to a home improvement project (although here, a drains up approach might be applicable). Why do we do it at work?

> "My biggest bugbear is the use of action as a verb. It is quite clearly a noun. It is one of those ones that is never used outside work. I have never asked my wife if she would like me to 'action' a cup of tea for her." International publisher

> "Nobody ever uses these phrases at home. So at night you are able to say to your spouse and family 'no problem, I will call the plumbers tomorrow and see if they have any idea about the leaking tap', yet in the bright daylight it becomes 'I'll be sure to reach out to the facilities team and see if we can schedule a deep dive into the ongoing liquidity issues.'" International strategy executive.

To return to the song:

Be a mat nor a mouse
When you shout 'House!'
What're you trying to really say?
When you use the lingua franca
You become a corporate wanker
It's just sweet FA.

CHAPTER 3
WHY DO WE DO IT?

> "I HATE corporate jargon. And, unsurprisingly, being in an American company there's loads flying around. I really don't like being asked to 'loop' someone in. I don't really even know how I would go about it anyway as I was never very good at knots in Cubs. But I think my least favourite phrase (or the one I love to hate the most) is 'low hanging fruit'. Weirdly, it's actually longer to say than what it replaces, which I guess is 'quick win.'"
> UK head of communications for US-headquartered firm

I HAVE a number of theories why we might feel the need to scatter these idioms and expressions throughout our business and social lives.

Reflecting on my early PR career, when we took the conscious decision to compete with management consultants by speaking their own language, there was a sense of camaraderie in sharing a language we enjoyed using. We felt part of a club, part of a group of elite business advisors identified by our badge of seemingly clever jargon.

Young, blinding and cutting edge?

We believed that we were part of the smart club. Young, up-and-coming smart[-arsed[7]] executives and professionals. We truly believed that by bamboozling and blinding our clients with our business terminology, they would listen, awestruck by our awesomeness[8]. This is what we believed. Then we stopped to listen a bit more. After all, isn't that what consultants are supposed to do? Listen first, consider and then respond? I once heard a head of sales of a financial services clearing firm explain to her team: "There's a reason why we have two ears and one mouth – so we hear more than we speak." To her credit, she admitted the cheesiness of her observation, but she had a good point – the importance of listening to clients. Wind back to my early PR days, when listening to our clients, it dawned on us that they too were adopting this mystical language. Why? Were they competing with their agency, keeping up with their agency or falling into a similar trap? Perhaps a case of 'if you can't beat them, join them'? Many firms view one of the benefits of hiring a PR firm is to keep up with the latest developments so that internally they would appear well informed and *cutting edge*. Bandying around these expressions would make them sound pretty cool, of the moment and, quite frankly, *street*.

Truth be told, we were all feeling pretty bloody pleased with ourselves. We truly believed that we were a cut above the rest, as we scattered expressions and added value ad nauseam. We probably even felt a little smug when another person in the meeting let slip that they did not understand what we meant. We interpreted their raised eyebrows as meaning 'if only we were as smart as you', when in hindsight they probably thought we were pretentious 'bankers'.

---

7   The word arsed inserted appropriately in 2012, some 20 years later.

8   The word awesome inserted inappropriately in 2012, some 20 years later – fortunately no-one said awesome in 1992 so that is a blessing at least. I shudder to think of needing to tolerate the next 20 years of inevitable awesomeness.

One very senior executive at an international PR firm, and someone I have always held in highest esteem as one who spoke plainly, clearly and with the greatest authority, offers an explanation: "I reckon corporate speak is something you learn on your way up the greasy pole and reaches its peak as a disease when you are in your mid-thirties. After that, you either atrophy, frozen by your buzzwords – or you discard it in search of simplicity. I hope I'm in the latter category." He certainly is.

And isn't that exactly the point?

It still goes on. Young bright, up-and-coming executives don the shoes we have worn through. As an older fuddy-duddy forty-something, have I simply outgrown the language?

As part of my research, I asked an executive coach who works with clients across Europe whether she had heard any new expressions. She responded: "Nothing new – all the same old same old – but said by the young and keen as though they thought them up for themselves ..."

I mentioned about wanting to illustrate that we are 'of the moment'. The emergence of new expressions continues and always will. As we work our 9-5[9] jobs, somewhere in the world someone is conjuring up '*put it in your mindwok and stir it*' and then '*we'll socialise the idea*' and if we want to '*run with the big dogs*' we'll have to '*kill some puppies*' and deal with the '*broken biscuits*'? Oh sorry, that's '*my bad*' because '*normilarily*' in this competitive world of '*dog eat sushi*' I am just a '*small fish in the foot spa of life*'. Ok, I confess that the last three are my inventions, but the others aren't, which makes mine seem entirely plausible. [10] And yes, the puppy murder IS a used expression. I know, just imagine the eyes.

---

9   If only.

10 I used 'normilarily' once in conversation with a colleague: 'well norminarily, this is what we should do'. We both stopped in our tracks and for a few seconds couldn't figure out what was wrong with the sentence. Normilarily seemed to fit, although not – as we agreed – ever to be repeated.

Innovation breeds jargon

Technology and innovation create new expressions and terminology. Working with entrepreneurs of technology firms or heads of technology of more established firms, one of their greatest challenges is to describe what on earth they mean without being dragged down by a mass of acronyms and technology jargon. And by the way, *paradigm shifting, leading provider of cutting edge*, and *best of breed solutions* means nothing.

As a financial technology journalist put it to me: "We are a leading provider of XXX solutions" is the second most annoying expression, right behind 'we are almost unique in the respect that....'"

(Oh, and as an aside, I do think that every publication should follow the lead of the *Wall Street Journal Europe* which employs a technology and innovation correspondent called Chip. Brilliant.)

Another US-based journalist concurred: "The most irritating expression that springs to mind for me is the use of the word 'leading'. Everything is the leading software provider or leading broker-dealer or leading consultancy. Leading by what measure? Some of the firms that make this claim are tiny ones that you've never heard of, proving that 'leading' is absolutely meaningless."

Instead, we are finding that technology firms are finding new ways to describe what they do. They talk about incubators and ecosystems – nothing to do with premature babies or climate controlled environments. Data is big and everyone's heads are in the clouds. I am sure that IT helpdesks take great joy in advising us to *power up and power down* instead of switching the computer off and on again. IT language is a language of its own and all I have to say to that is 11001101101. I do, however, really like PICNIC – '*Problem is Clearly Not In Computer*', meaning the problem is between the keyboard and the chair.

WHY DO WE DO IT?

Technology is full of jargon – bandwidth, redundancy, latency, frequency, backbones. Where will it end? Technology breeds terminology. Forget Moore's Law, which was described to me as meaning that the processing speeds and power of technology doubles every two years. Streets' Law suggests that every two years the amount of jargon doubles. [11]

Trying to explain how the technology helps non-technology people requires a stripping-out of jargon, set to make any CTO twitch. At the start of any project with a technology client, I use a highly sophisticated technique I call the 'belligerent teenager'. As the client explains the features and benefits, I listen intently and when I hear anything littered with jargon reserve the right to respond with 'yeah, but so what', 'so why should I care', 'what's in it for me?'. Technology in itself is not appealing. What your technology can do for me to make my life easier is.

Businesses create their own. Processes create their own – for example, anyone who has been through a merger and acquisition may well have been 'TUPED'. This is a verb from the Transfer of Undertakings Protection of Employment Legislation, an important part of UK labour law designed to protect employees whose business is being transferred to another business.

A friend of mine who works for a global automotive firm wrote:

> "The only gripe here is about abbreviations. [Really, the only gripe? Either the firm is impressive or the employees very tolerant!] We use loads of these. TME, TMME, TMUK, TGB, TFS, TDG, TMS and so it goes on. That's just in the office. In the cars it gets better: VSC, ABS, DAB, MPV, LHD, DNA (yes, we actually use that term when referring to vehicles, sad but true), LED DRL, USB, e-CVT, EV, ECO, NVH, oh nearly forgot...VSC+, HAC, EPS, EBD,

---

[11] And why can't I have a law? Did Moore have to go through any legislative rubber-stamping?

BA, TRC, PWR. These I have taken from just one of our 'quick guides' for one model and a rather lovely model to boot ..."

Wow. Clearly anticipating my next question (I would have said pre-empting, but persevere with the book and you'll understand why I backed away), he added: "Please do not ask me what they all mean, as I only know a few. I've only been here 10 years!"

Language tribes

We use these corporate expressions in an effort to fit in. I have read many media articles about business language. One which particularly stands out for me was written by Alina Dizik in the Wall Street Journal which sheds some light on why jargon and business slang is important. In an article published in May 2012 entitled 'Mastering the Finer Points of American Slang', Ms Dizik interviewed entrepreneur Gaurav Dhy, in Wellesley, Massachusetts. Mr Dhy studied English in his native India, but when he moved to Boston he realised he had a great deal to learn about the way Americans speak if he wanted to fit in. This particularly affected pre-business small talk in meetings.

Learning American idioms has been challenging enough, but texting, email and social networks have generated a tidal wave of new slang and abbreviations. It is hard enough to get to grips with texting shorthand including 'OMG' (Oh my God), 'BFF' (Best Friend Forever) and the others which are emerging, including 'LMK' (let me know), 'YOLO' (you only live once), 'ROFL' (rolling on floor laughing) or, as newswire journalist recently wrote, 'IMHO' (in my humble opinion). In addition to mastering this mobile – or should I say 'cell' vernacular, Ms Dizik explained how Mr Dhy also had to tackle appropriate linguistic nuances; for example, why it is acceptable to say 'fail', but he should avoid use of the word 'failure'? Clichés and idioms play a role in our efforts to fit in. We have to admit that the line between fitting in and trying too hard to fit in is very fine. Only please don't ask because we cannot actually explain where it is drawn. All-too-eager efforts by one person may fail if met with a scepticism by the other party that they are trying too hard. It is a social minefield. In the glossary, I warn about the potential pitfall of balls, bucks and bottoms. Each is central to many expressions, but muddle them up and the consequences could be unfortunate.

Television programmes also create new expressions. The popular US sitcom 'Friends' started the trend of entering a room to a greeting of 'hey' instead of hello. In the UK, TV shows like 'The Only Way is Essex' (itself responsible for the abbreviation used as an expression, 'so TOWIE') has brought to light new expressions such as 'well jel' (very jealous) and 'reem' (no idea – no really, I actually have no idea what that is supposed to mean – cool, maybe?) If you hear these expressions in a meeting, distance yourself immediately and avoid the temptation to use them, the response will be far from totes amazeballs.

I am amused by Ms Dizik's reference to one Amy Gillet, an author of English slang and idiom vocabulary books. She is quoted in the context of choosing which words and phrases are appropriate for the speaker and the situation. She teaches international business students that it is fine to use 'slacking off' and refer to being 'stressed out', but then says that she stops short of teaching idioms that are too 'cutting edge' (her words or the journalist's, I'm not sure), such as using 'sick' to mean 'cool' – yes, I get that – or 'epic' to mean 'awesome'. Really? So, teaching 'awesome' is acceptable?[12]

And so to the US influence.

We cannot avoid this *elephant in the room*. Secretly, we Brits have admired the exotic language used by Americans, includ-

---

12 On the subject of epic, is it me or everything turning epic? To my mind the expression was coined to describe adventure films but apparently insurance can make me feel epic as can crinkled crisps. Who knew?

ing those which have pervaded business language. We have loved and happily adopted their baseball expressions (a relatively small sample of which are listed in the Appendix to the glossary). *Covering our bases* after we've touched them, and throwing *curve balls* while *stepping up to the plate to hit a home run* have given us decades of pleasure. If only it were true the other way around. Do we believe that US executives talk about 'leg before wickets', 'scoring a rounder' or – and I would love for this to start being used –' I think you'll find you're well and truly croqueted'. Hmm, perhaps not.

There is also a question of speed. Rather than use longer-winded explanations, shorter ones are used instead. Why would you communicate a longer concept when a shorter explanation would suit better? We live in a world of social media driven by status updates and 140 character tweets. Understand it or not, like it or not, every business falls under its influence in one way or another. In social media, every opportunity for abbreviation can only help, IMHO. But this isn't a recent phenomenon; knowingly or not, we've been doing it for years. We drill down, rather than look at something in detail, or refer to an offsite rather than a meeting held away from the office premises. However, brevity can frustrate. As a senior and seasoned PR training and development professional explained it to me: "When we're talking about other people 'eating our lunch' this is really no shorter than 'taking our businesses', so why do it?" And while we're at it, why do we say 'fess up' instead of 'confess' – it is no shorter.

It's not all about knowing it all

I have observed how idioms and expressions are often used to compensate for or cover up a lack of knowledge. This can be very common in the management consultancy, PR, marketing and communications sectors, but I certainly wouldn't limit it to those industries. It is a natural – and false – expectation that we should know the answer to everything, yet we do not need to know the answer to everything. I am certainly sceptical of anyone who believes they have an answer for everything, and there are plenty of people like this out there. We should know what we know, know what we don't know and know how best to find out. Having asked the right questions to find out what we do need to know, we then decide what best to do, and that is when we start advising. But yet, rather than be afraid to ask the questions to find out what we need to know, we face a temptation and tendency to just talk and talk and talk and talk and talk, wrapping ourselves up in tentacles of jargon almost to the point of strangulation. If we don't strangle ourselves, the chances are someone else at the table will want to do it to us.

I would argue that does very little for either the client, the consultant or the outside world. I have also worked on the client side and hired consultants in the UK and across Europe. As a client, we do not expect you to understand everything. We expect you to know how to ask the smart questions and generate appropriate ideas to help us achieve our objectives.

Present, presentable and presence

I appreciate that this is slight deviation from the premise of this book, but I am asked quite frequently for advice I would give any young person trying to progress their career in these competitive and economically challenging times.

A recent example was an invitation I accepted to be Guest Speaker at my Old School, Walthamstow Hall in Sevenoaks, Kent. My challenge was to offer advice to a group of school-leavers about how they might stand apart from their peers in a competitive world. Before I spoke, the audience had patiently sat through three speeches before mine and I needed to be as brief and as engaging as possible. I wanted to offer them some advice in a way they might remember! In making presentations, public speaking and comedy, three is the magic number and I adopted this approach. I suggested that beyond being as well qualified as they possibly could become, in order to stand out they need to be present, be presentable and have presence. Briefly, here's what I mean, which is also an extension of my earlier point about people doing business with people they like.

By **present** I mean turn up on time, preferably a little early, work hard, demonstrate an interest in your role and how it fits in, in your colleagues and the progress of the division and firm.

Being **presentable** means groomed and appropriately dressed. This may sound obvious, but it is amazing how often people get this wrong.

Having **presence**. It's not all about you. One of the most effective ways of making an impact is to take an interest in others. When you talk to someone, talk to them square on, not with an eye constantly over their shoulder. Have a good firm handshake and make eye contact. (Quick tip – just focus on one eye, and it is fine to blink – otherwise you run the risk of appearing slightly demonic.) Demonstrate that you have listened and are interested in what the other person has to say by asking questions.

Treat everyone with respect – how you would like to be treated yourself – and be as apolitical as you possibly can be, hard as it may be on some days. Be positive, but not to the point of the irritating or ridiculous. Do it all with a sense of humour, a sense of humility and a sense of grace. I believe this will make you indispensable.

Speaking their language

OK, back to why we use corporate expressions. (Thank you for indulging me.)

Sometimes we just don't realise that we are using them. My brother works in advertising and I joke in my show about the true occasion when we were planning a day out around his daughter's eating and sleeping routine. He said, 'I think that between 10 and 11 we will have a window of feeding opportunity'. When I pulled him on it and pointed out that he sounded a bit of a 'banker', he genuinely couldn't see what he had done or why I had pointed it out.

More than that, we are now mixing our idioms. It's not uncommon that we hear people 'misabuse' these expressions. It's not 'rocket surgery'. One of my clients explained that they have been keeping a record of expressions and he invited me to take a look at the hallowed pages of the book. I particularly liked the mixed idioms which include: 'What time is a piece of string'; 'I can see the carrot at the end of the tunnel'; 'It's a doubled headed sword' and 'I can't tell you ... Chinese windows'.

My frustration with corporate expressions may be justified but I fear – actually I know – that I am fighting a lost cause. I am *wading through treacle, swimming against the tide and pushing water uphill.*

I will never win this battle, because new ones are being invented all the time. As I write, I am sitting in a coffee shop in London. Within earshot is a group of six Americans. I can't quite figure out what they do, they could be young programmers or 'creatives'. They have repeated a number of times the roles of their colleagues, calling them 'imagineers' and 'fungineers'. Seeing this is in writing suggests to me that John, the 'Chief Fungineer' to whom they refer, is scientifically creating a mushroom. (Or a drug scorer.)

We write differently today. Infinitives split; we end sentences in ways my English Literature teacher would be furious with. OK, with which my English Literature teacher would be furious (I can hear her now). New generations of executives are coming through the education system, taught by teachers who teach differently from those who taught them. We are less formal. It is increasingly rare for me to refer to a business contact by their surname, or should I say family name? Channels of communication – by which I mean computers, television, even that we speak over the internet not just the telephone – and specialist groups influence and change how we write and speak. Over time we have become accustomed to hearing expressions we would never have heard a few months or years ago. In this day and age of tablet, social and internet-enabled technology, we are used to hearing expressions, clueless about what they really mean or how they work. And do you know what? That's fine. I don't want, or need, to know what makes the app icons wiggle on my tablet. And if you want to get in touch, you can friend or like me on Facebook [13].

Industries, sectors and social groups create expressions. I have little doubt that Sudoku fan clubs have jargon of their own, as do lawyers, accountants and medics. All I would argue is that in all communication we 'know our audience'. Each and every person will have different level of understanding and it can change by the smallest degree. I can't 'poke' my mother, but I can meet my father 'in the cloud'.

---

13 I'd love to hear from you on my page: The Lingua Franca of the Corporate Banker.

CHAPTER 4
I AM NOT ALONE

By now you will have picked up on my resigned irritation. I felt only right to gauge the sentiment of others. I had a feeling that people would find corporate jargon exasperating and I expected them to scoff mildly at some of the silliness of the expressions. I based this not only on conversations with friends, family and business contacts, but also on media articles on the subject of corporate jargon. Over the years there have been many articles published about office annoyances. One I particularly noted was published in February 2010 by Reuters, the news service. It was entitled 'Does 'thinking outside the box' drive you mad?'

The top 10 office irritations

The article ranked office jargon[14] fourth behind grumpy colleagues, which took top position, slow computers, then small talk/gossip in the office in a list of office annoyances in a survey of 'workers'. (Forget associates. Workers. Not even co-workers.)
    It is worth looking at the rest of the league table.

    5.   People speaking loudly on the phone
    6.   Too much health and safety in the workplace
    7.   Poor toilet etiquette
    8.   People not turning up for meetings on time or at all

---

14 Survey by Opinium Research of 1,836 people.

9. People not tidying up after themselves in the kitchen
10. Too cold/ cold air conditioning

According to Reuters, nearly two-thirds of respondents said their stress levels had been increased by office irritations and one in 10 had left a job because of them.

For me, writing this has been a bit of a cathartic outlet for my frustration, but I can't imagination a situation where I would be driven to leaving a job over excessive use of corporate jargon.

But feelings ride high and I was quite bowled over by the reactions I received.

Top ranking irritating jargon

I was keen to solicit answers to two key questions of my colleagues and friends. I call it research, others call it 'crowdsourcing'. I asked two simple questions:

Question One: Which expression(s) irritates you the most when you hear it used? If more than one, please rank in order of most irritating first.

Question Two: Have you heard any new expressions recently? If so, what are they?

The responses came in thick and fast.

Some people repeated the expressions they disliked in the form of encouragement: "Best of luck leveraging your core capabilities and going after this low hanging fruit", wrote one newswire journalist from New York.

Others replied with great gusto. One head of policy for a government agency replied: "OMG. I'm going to have to workshop this upload to be able to even get my head around the overall topic, let alone parameterise the sort of area in which the conceptual solution might, as a ballpark, lie. So. Let me try and organise my thoughts. It usually helps me to knock up a few slides and maybe present back to you what a sample business model or two might look like. Important to know what good looks like."

The CEO of one of my global clients responded: "You've crossed the rubicon with this email. It's not in the domain of our firm's terms of reference. We need a drains up meeting on this. At this meeting we'll shake the tree to see how the leaves fall. Depending on the outcome we may need to escalate to high echelons for powerthoughting."

They clearly were taking great joy in constructing the most ridiculous collection of sentences in response. But they make a good point; it may be an imaginative slight stretch beyond the realistic, but not a stretch too far.

Many wrote back to tell me how much they 'hate' marketing jargon! Much language was too colourful to repeat as I was bombarded with pent-up frustration.

A commercial director of a publishing house vented: "I despise 'at the end of the day' ... It is not the end of the day and stop speaking in clichés, it is annoying. 'To be fair' – no, you are not trying to be fair, you are lying to me and now I have proof! 'With respect' – mmmm no, now I know that you have no respect for me or the business we are trying to do, you are in fact a liar and a poor one, 'with respect'. 'Negative growth' – do you mean shrinkage? Because either it gets bigger or it gets smaller, it does not get negatively bigger. Idiot – negative growth is physically impossible; physically in both the biological sense and in relation to physics; as in the laws of."

And breathe!

One London-based international bond trader wrote back: "I really enjoyed writing these phrases down, feels like psychotherapy." And then went on to use it as opportunity to vent a frustration which frankly should be right up there on the Reuters' list of office annoyances. "I have an aversion to noisy eaters and people with bad eating habits. That more and more people eat at their desk has led to me being constantly 'under attack". There was the carrot cruncher who sat opposite me; he ate a carrot a day, every day for four years. I wanted to kill him. Then there was the American colleague who used to eat with his mouth open; going to a business lunch with him used to be like watching a washing machine turning clothes round and round – yuk. I currently sit next to a 'food mumbler'; he usually chooses to speak when he has half a bacon sandwich in his mouth – horrible. Anyway, I should get out of the office as lunchtime is approaching and I don't want to be here when people start eating. It's the reason I run at lunchtimes (well, one of them)."

Who can blame him? But let's return to the matter in hand.

A software technology marketing manager told me: "Two particular bugbears over the years are 'blue sky thinking' and 'let's take it back to grass roots level' – why not just say it as it is!"

"By a mile, 'de minimis' is the most f**king annoying term at present, when people just mean minimal or minor", vented the editor of a fund management publication. "Presumably users think Latin makes them sound important. Grrr. Oh yes, and 'perfect storm'. When there's more than one cause to an outcome suddenly it's a perfect bloody storm. Annoying through overuse."

One event manager in London went as far as to share a brief she had received. I am told this is provided verbatim:

> "This event will act as a strategic platform for Innovation, Skills and Education, Creativity, Collaboration and Thought Leadership in the creative broadcast, media and technology ecosystem. The event will comprise of a Conference, Collaborative Sessions, an Expo for partners, Live Experiences.
>
> The main Objectives are:
> 1. A better connected, collaborative ecosystem that benefits all.

2. The establishment of a climate that encourages learning and sharing.
3. Development of truly converged solutions that anticipate and deliver upon customer needs.
4. Renewed hunger for innovation.

It went on …"

She adds, "I think my particular favourites are 'strategic platform', 'truly converged solutions' and anything that includes the word 'hunger'. Well quite, and frankly, who wouldn't benefit from a better connected, collaborative ecosystem that benefits all?"

A journalist singled out a three-letter word which drives him to distraction. "Top of the list though must be abuse of the poor suffix 'pre'. I don't know what it did wrong, but it gets misused appallingly every day. I think it started in the business world, but one can hardly find a better example to illustrate how poor corporate language can spread if not stamped on straight away. People use it all the time without considering what they say. 'We're having a pre-meeting.' What? You're having a meeting before the meeting? Or just a meeting?

'Pre-order/pre-book' – I think you'll find you're just booking or ordering something. You just don't receive it instantly. Unless I missed something and you're ordering before ordering. I'm ordering the latest Harry Potter book, published in September. I'm not pre-ordering it. It's marketing hype, ladies and gents.

'Prequel' – an abomination of the English language that should result in an electric shock to sensitive parts to anyone, man or woman, caught using it."

The next time I saw him he asked how the book was progressing. Near completion I told him, we were planning the marketing and had decided to pre-launch it. Let's just say that I received the reaction I was hoping for!

This journalist emailed a number of times. Also high on his list of irritating expressions sits 'meet/meet with'. He explains: "Meet will do most of the time, the word implies you're coming into contact with someone. It's a pretty critical part of its definition. There is a place for use of 'with', just not 99 per cent of the time it is used." The irritations just kept coming. Another dislike lay with the continued misspelling of focussed (vs focused) and the use of 'outturn' to describe a financial result. "No, it's either revenues or profits, the rest is deliberate obfuscation."

My world does extend beyond the media and financial services and a director of a social care trust wrote to tell me that 'at the end of the day' was most frustrating expression. 'At the end of the day, it is night - get over it', she wrote. She added, "It is unbelievable how many time you hear the phrase 'bear with me' when you speak to someone on the phone. A pyschotherapist friend always quickly retorts 'quick, run away – they're very dangerous!' This always amuses me and have tried it myself – not one person has ever realised what I have said, or get it!"

Economic with invention

New ones are being formed on a daily basis. A senior investment manager pointed me to references to 'Grexit' (the potential departure of Greece from the European Union). The state of the Greek economy is a major factor, as the UK is dipping in and out of a reported second recession, depending on who you believe. People like to refer to the 'double dip' recession. I call it the 'taramasalata dip' recession. The investment manager's list continued with 'Spanick', a new expression invented out of concern for a potential Spanish default, suggesting that we face the possibility of a Squit (Spain quitting the Euro). Clearly, the politicians need to 'concretise' – as a stock exchange sales executive put it me – their austerity plans.

In the world of stock trading, new expressions are being invented. We live in a world where we talk about 'best execution'. Put aside any visions of competing guillotines in an effort to reduce headcount in the world of trading. It means getting the best possible trading result. Traders talk of 'arbitrage opportunities' and invent new terminology. The head of PR of one of our clients pointed me to an article by Tom Steinert-Threlkeld in the online trading publication, Securities Technology Monitor. In June 2012 Mr Steinert-Threlkeld wrote an article about new trading terminology entitled 'Who says all financial and trading terms have to be baragouin (gibberish)?' He lists a number of expressions including:

Garbatrage – Stocks that rise because of a major takeover of an unrelated entity. These stocks do not have any significant involvement in the target corporation or in its industry. Hence, they have no real reason to rise.

Rumourtrage – The buying and selling of securities based on the rumour of a takeover.

He lists exotic expressions including 'spoofing' and 'dead cross', technical trading terms which will cause you to glaze over. For example, a dead cross is a crossover resulting from a security's long-term moving average breaking above its short term moving average or support level. I did warn you.

Some have made it into everyday conversation, for example a 'dead cat bounce'. Dead cat bounce – which I am told has been around for at least a decade – is used to describe a brief market rally after a prolonged fall. If there has been no change in underlying sentiment, the rally will be followed by renewed weakness. It is derived from the notion that even a dead cat bounces if dropped from a great height. I confess that I didn't think this what it meant at all. I thought it meant that as more of feline splat – or cat splat – causing entrails to explode on impact with the pavement. I thought a dead cat bounce meant that it is game over, pack your bags, it is time to get out. How wrong was I? It is encouraging to know that things are not as bad as I first thought.

From my months of hoarding expressions, secretly noting them during meetings and asking around, I thought I had a pretty good sense of what is bandied around in the big, bad world of business. I thought I was pretty well networked and connected, but as you will have seen from the job titles of the respondents, my circles are limited. I fully expected that other businesses and sectors would have their own, but there were some I didn't see coming.

A country manager for a poker company told me that "We aim to implement a pitcher-catcher strategy". She explained, "We pitch the idea, catch it and run. Yeah baby!" When I mentioned this one to a journalist he pointed out this as "Also gibberish! You can't pitch, catch and run. You're either pitching, catching or running."

A policy manager in the private sector told me that her colleagues have been known to talk about broken biscuits, that from time to time you have to kill some puppies and referring to conditions as being NFN (Normal for Norfolk). I looked this up on the 'Literary Norfolk' website which, without hint of shame or irony, informed me that this was created by doctors at the Norfolk and Norwich hospital to categorise some of their more 'intellectually challenged' patients. The term was then abbreviated to NFN. My policy manager friend told me she had heard this term being used in business to describe someone perceived as intellectually challenged. I recounted this to another friend who responded with "Oh, a bit like FLK?" My blank expression clearly warranted further explanation. "Funny looking kid", he said. As my eyebrows raised, he expanded "Only when there's no reason for them to look funny." Oh, that's fine then.

The lunchtime office-evading bond trader gave me his three newly irritating expressions:

1. 'Value engineering'. "I am hearing this more and more. 'This proposal needs some value engineering'. It basically translates as we 'need to cut costs'."
2. 'Enterprise solutions'. "A term made up by marketing guys to enhance interest in business proposals made to clients. It means absolutely nothing."
3. 'Peace'. "A few people sign off with the word 'Peace' instead of 'Regards' and it annoys the hell out of me."

"My personal gripe is the recent rise of 'Sorry … my bad' – I hate that", said a senior equities trader. A senior marketing consultant in NY agreed "I hate the phrase 'my bad', when what they mean is 'my mistake' or 'my error'". She added, "I also hate 'I heart' something – just say 'I love'."

The national journalist, who hates the abuse of 'pre', wrote a third time to add 'future proofing' to his list. "I mean, just what the hell is that? You waterproof tangible stuff, like a roof or a basement. How do you proof against something intangible? You've managed to make time stop so it'll never affect you or your business? Even if you don't take it literally, are you telling me you're so all-seeing and all-knowing you've thought of absolutely everything? That it's not going to be superseded by future tech developments? Like Betamax, like VHS video. It is literal nonsense and figuratively, arrogant tosh." Enough said.

A UK editor of a banking technology title sent me an anecdote: "I have an ancient treasure from a digital equipment press conference in 1981. Trying to herd the hacks (journalists) back on the timetable, a flustered flack (PR officer) announced 'owing to time criticality, we must proceed fastly'. We spent the rest of the trip inventing new names for things – a staircase became an 'incremental ascent/descent walkway' and a comb was a, 'interstitial cranial keratinised tissue manipulation device' or some such."

I loved that. It reminds me of pro-pixel intensifying faux-tanical hydro-jargon microbead extra featuring nutritive volumizing technology. Better known as moisturising cream.

'Let's workshop it' was flagged by a CEO of financial services consultancy as she pointed out that "workshop appears to have become a verb". She admitted to being slightly bamboozled by 'quarterbacking – who's going to quarterback this project?' Adding, "It's lingo for project manage – I think!"

A private wealth investment manager kindly sent me a substantial list of new expressions she had heard. I couldn't include them all and lifted out the ones I (dis)liked the most. Scarily, I realised that I could simply join them all together to make some form of nonsensical diatribe: The sidecar of your question is to try to make a big thing not too big because even the best surfer needs a good wave. Besides, build a seawall, don't leave it until the storm is over and it is important to know which levers to pull to make it fly because it's growing at a fast clip. It's my bad, I can't kill it off so I suggest we pop it on a post-it and come back to it later, because at the end of the day it's looking frothy.

A Moscow-based account director of an international financial firm wrote, "I hate, I loathe the two following: 'leverage' instead of 'use' and 'going forward' instead of 'in the future'."

A colleague at Streets Consulting told me she had received a mailer about the mix of PR and marketing – it's called PRketing. Seriously? And while I am at it, I saw recently that a PR firm was hiring an 'office procedures assistant'. What the hell is that? Do you need an assistant to help you follow the procedures of an office? Can't you do it yourself?

'I can't process all of this so I'm putting it in my mindwok and stirring', added the CEO of a global brokerage firm. But one thing is for sure, we need to put a pin in it (in the bursting, not defining, sense). This book serves as my opportunity to burst the balloon because as a senior regulatory specialist reminded me 'you have the pen'.

When it feels like you can't go on

I ranked the responses because you can't beat a good ranking. I wasn't surprised to have received so many replies with expressions that others hadn't sent; there are over 500 in the glossary after all. That said, there were three runaway winners and flushed with the Olympic success of Team GB, it seems only fitting to place these on a 'Lingua Franca Podium of Irritation'. I started out with bronze, silver and gold awards but this didn't seem fitting and settled with 3rd, 2nd and 1st.

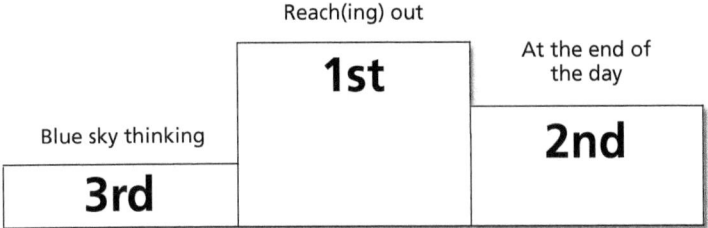

The third most irritating was 'blue sky thinking', followed by 'at the end of the day', but the runaway winner by a huge margin was 'reaching out'.

A senior sales executive at a stockbroking firm replied: "The worst, by a mile, are 'stretch the envelope' and 'reach out', particularly when said by an American in NY to me in London … how long are his arms??!!"

Opening the kimono on your sweet spot?

For me, 'opening the kimono' and 'sweet spot' are right up there on the league table of annoying new expressions. I was recently in a client meeting negotiating a contract. When we came to the critical fee negotiation moment, the client looked at me with a dead set expression and said: "I guess this is the moment where we open our kimonos". Eeew. As the future-proof, pre-protecting national journalist pointed out "it misunderstands the nature of the word". He's right – a kimono involves enormous lengths of cloth which take a long time to assemble and requires extraordinary skill. To open a kimono would take forever.

My toe-curled reaction to kimono opening only worsened when, within a matter of minutes, he had asked me where my sweet spot was. I recounted this story to a friend over a glass of white from further down the wine list – a good measure of any career progression – and asked her where her sweet spot was. In a flash she replied "at the cheese counter in Waitrose".

Kimono opening leads me to a delicate section. Inappropriate innuendo. One freelance journalist suggested I should dedicate a chapter to macho and sexual language. "In sales, people talk about eating what you kill, penetration and brand stickiness." In reference to being 'screwed' over price, I once heard a sales director refer to bending over and dropping their trousers for the clients. Not only was I surprised at the choice of words, I was intrigued by why she would feel the need to use sexually machismo language. It is not that I am prudish, more baffled.

Combine this with kimono opening, sweet spots, sucking and seeing and big swinging dicks (which, as the journalist commented, conjures up an unpleasant mental image of "some sort of fleshy wind-chime!") and I think that's more than enough, thank you. Oh – it turns out I was wrong, evidently I am a prude. Oh well.

Drinking the Kool Aid

In January 2012, *Forbes* magazine published an article entitled 'The most annoying pretentious and useless business jargon' on its website. It invited readers to vote for their most annoying expression.

Daily for 32 days, *Forbes* pitted two expressions against each other and readers voted using Twitter. The goal was to identify the single most annoying example of business jargon and thoroughly embarrass all who employ it. The winner of each match-up (for example, 'reach out' vs 'it is what it is') was taken forward to another match-up for the reader's vote. Think of it as a jargon-off (given that anything which involves a head-to-head competition these days seems to be a something-off – I once witnessed two friends have a cake-off – that was quite a sight). At the end, having seen off many other contenders, 'leverage' was a finalist pitted against 'drinking the Kool Aid'. Kool Aid readers tweeted and was declared the winner – or should I say, loser?

It would be remiss of me to ever consider writing a book about corporate language without referring to the doyenne of corporate observation, Lucy Kellaway at the *Financial Times*. As avid readers will know, Ms Kellaway is known for serving up no-nonsense observation of corporate and management behaviour in her weekly column.

In a column published in the midst of the 'swine flu' epidemic in October 2009, Ms Kellaway observed how firms were reminding employees how to wash their hands. Her column suggested that firms should 'Wash away the verbal germs of management speak' and with good reason. She wrote that she had come across use of 'hygiene' as a description for the optimal amount of working capital on an organisation's balance sheet. She mocked a book which referred to good employees as "top talent", "high echelon employees", "high potential talent", "high octane brainpower" and even "the delta force of the workplace". Ms Kellaway called for a clean-up of "these verbal germs that must be flushed down the lavatory with a large glug of bleach poured in afterwards to prevent further infection." She argued that, rather than the recession killing off "the global epidemic of Waffle Flu … it continues to infect increasing numbers of the business population, interfering with the functioning of the brain, and sometimes leaving the patient unable to communicate at all." In response to her article, I sent her the lyrics to my song 'Bullshit Bingo' under the subject line of 'Waffle flu to music'. Only imagining how busy she must be, I didn't expect a response and was delighted when she kindly replied:

> 09/09/2009 (interesting, I had never noticed the date until now)
>
> *"Dear Julia*
>
> Liked that v much indeed ... am almost humming myself...
>
> *Lucy"*

I realise of course that this sounds incredibly sycophantic. I'm not ashamed. I'm rather proud.

But there is good news. While we are creating new ones, it has also occurred to me that others are ebbing away. Less and less we hear people use A1 or A-OK and it has been a long time since I have heard someone in business use the very annoying 'Wayne's World' abomination of reversing the meaning of a comment by adding 'NOT!' at the end.

I'm hoping others will simply Wayne away.

CHAPTER 5
BULLSHIT BINGO

I HAVE MENTIONED my song, which I also perform as poetry for those occasions when a guitar seems out of place. Over the years, I have run offsite meetings for clients and when the hard work is done I serve up comedy as drinks are served up for the delegates. Some firms have even commissioned a song designed to include some light management lampooning. As I pull out the guitar, I can't help feel like a cross between Ricky Gervais' character David Brent from the TV show 'The Office' and Val Doonican. In one episode, David Brent brings in a facilitator to run a training session and, despite the best efforts of the training professional, the session is sabotaged by David Brent playing 'Freelove Freeway' on his guitar. In my show, I comment about how references to Val Doonican make you feel old. I took my team to a bar one evening and as I hopped on the bar stool I said "I feel a bit like Val Doonican", to which one member said "Who's she?"[15]

Oddness aside, when I perform 'Bullshit Bingo' I am always delighted when people approach me afterwards. It never fails to amuse me – not least given the size of the glossary in this book – when they tell me most emphatically that I have missed one.

---

15 Doonican is an Irish singer, also known as a 'crooner'. He was a regular fixture on BBC Saturday TV in the 1970s. Saturday nights have never been the same since.

Whatever the industry, the reality is that all business people are aware of the ridiculousness of the jargon, probably use it themselves (although don't always admit it) and ridicule it when others serve it up to them. I knew that the concept of 'bullshit bingo' or 'buzzword bingo', as was popularised by the Dilbert cartoons, existed because I have played it and others have mentioned it. That was why I wrote the song. I did not, however, anticipate the number of stories I would be told about playing it.

When I first wrote the song, it fitted with a section in my comedy routine about playing corporate pranks. I talk about a fad in the mid-noughties (that wonderful expression for the first decade of the millennium which may now have crossed the line from wonderful expression to jargon, another fine line which is hard to define) which I first experienced when I was sitting in a meeting with my team. I said something (particularly insightful, naturally) and one of them leapt up, fists by their hips, simultaneously swinging their index finger out at me like they were pulling a gun from a holster, shouting "You're shootin' from the hip. I like your style." Immediately they sat down, returned their gaze to the agenda in front of them as though nothing had happened. A few minutes passed. I made another comment and someone else shot up from their chair and screamed "You. Are. On. Fire". And then sat down as though nothing had happened. I stopped the meeting and gently enquired from what frickin' planet had they landed?

An email was produced with a list of corporate pranks. This game of expression shouting with an abrupt return to normality was the first. The second was my favourite. Without telling anyone, switch the coffee in the office from caffeinated to decaffeinated. Let's face it, no-one will notice, they'll just be a bit sluggish for a bit. Wait three weeks, then switch it back. Genius! Imagine all these people sitting at their computers clicking their mice with caffeine-fuelled demonic digits.

The third on the email was play 'bullshit bingo'.

I come from the world of PR so as you can imagine, the world is full of them. I once witnessed a director say to a colleague without the slightest hint of irony "Trust me, I'm a doctor – I'm a spin doctor". But it is not only the preserve of PR people (or as I tongue-in-cheek call them 'PRtists' who create campaigns which will set the world on fire, also known as 'PRsonists').

These expressions exist in every industry. People use expressions like 'my door is always open' all the time. You should never trust anyone who tells you their door is always open, just like people who say 'let's touch base'. Well, you're not touching mine.

So to explain, Bullshit Bingo is best played alone undercover, but increasingly played in groups on conference calls where the other party can't see you.

The player draws a grid on a piece of paper. In each box they write an expression and when they hear someone use them, they cross it off. Once they have crossed off all of them, they leap to their feet, shout 'House!' and then sit down again as if nothing has happened.

I thought this was a rather dated game, despite the continued use of these expressions and invention of many, many, many more. In my conversations with colleagues and clients, I was surprised that many still play. I did not, however, anticipate the admittance of using pre-drawn grids, in-house applications designed by the IT department or using smart phone apps.

In most cases, bullshit bingo is played in secret. Mostly by a few employees as a bonding device to make fun of a corporate language abuser. It transpires this is not always the case. One very senior PR executive of a bank based in Canary Wharf (so that doesn't really narrow it down) told me that she used it as a mechanism to keep the staff alert and engaged on the compulsory and invariably long-winded global conference calls.

One friend hailing from the petroleum industry told me how they would play the game, but with a twist. Not only would you complete the grid and cross them off, but you had the opportunity to double your points. On conference calls with US colleagues, if you created a new expression and, using means foul(mouthed) or fair, could encourage your US counterpart to repeat it back, you doubled your score.

For example: a conference call between London and New York might proceed as follows:

NY: Hey London, how's it going?

London: Great, how's the weather? (I would imagine this would feature on the NY grid if they happened to be playing. It would be an easy point.)

NY: Not bad. How is it in London?

London: (prepared and poised) Well, it's really grey and wet – in fact (wait for it, wait for it) it's raining cats and lemons.

(some may end here but I'm told that the most savvy of players will enlist a colleague to help build it up)

London (colleague # 2): Oh my goodness, you won't believe it, I got drenched on my way in, it has been a while since it's been so wet like this – seriously cats and lemons.

(Three might be over-playing it, but some might give it a go for extra credibility – but I'm told only do this if you're experienced and have had some acting lessons)

London (colleague # 3): Not sure if you've heard but we're really struggling with drought conditions and it's only March so we shouldn't complain. Those cats and lemons are only helping my garden.

London (colleague # 2): That's true (subtle reaffirmation couched in conversational banter) ... anyway, so let's turn straight to the agenda.

[call continues to the distant sounds of box crossing as someone invariably says 'ticking all the boxes'.]

... So any other business?

London (colleage # 3): So Jon, when are you next planning to come to London?

NY: Well I've checked my schedule and the last week of April seems good.

London: Great we'll keep the date clear. Don't forget your umbrella.

NY: Good point, let's hope it's not raining cats and lemons (Bam! Double points!)

When I first heard this I was appalled!

OK, amused and appalled. More amused than appalled if I'm honest, but quite appalled nevertheless. It does entirely compound my point about taking advantage of a culture difference to literally score points. You wouldn't do it to a Spaniard, or an Italian – would you? Would you?

And yet every time I have told people this in the UK they have been amused, in the US appalled.

Fun as it might be to start a cross-pondal (should that be interdepondal? Or correspondal?) rivalry for conference calls and I would love to call on all my US contacts to join in, that would conflict with my central argument that communication should become simpler in the interests of corporate clarity, rather than encourage people to start new expressions.

What has surprised me is how many people have encouraged me to write this book, because of its two central premises – the interests of corporate communication simplicity and to provide a helpful and light-hearted glossary of terms.

"Remember Buzzword Bingo? Search Google/Wikipedia. It still exists and was actually a game invented in Silicon Valley, I believe, by the new age of techies – dotcom period

– no doubt as a part of their revolution against the staid corporate monoliths of the time. It went with the Hawaiian shorts they wore. And then they invented their own buzzwords to protect their new worlds."

Former Chairman and CEO of an international PR firm

I seem to have had a sheltered and rather straightforward career so far. I had no idea about other games out there.

An investment manager in London told me: "We have regular office meetings, which are broadcast to the rest of EMEA[16]. Should one of our colleagues be speaking, we come up with a word that they have to use when speaking, such as microwave or boggle. If they manage to fit it in to their speech we buy them lunch; if they fail, they have to buy a round of drinks at the next team night out!"

A charity fundraising officer told me that her father used to play 'Postcode Confusion'. He would slip in random postcodes into business conversations and see if people respond, e.g. "Well, I think what we need is an SG7..." or "The new NW2 model might be the best option ..."

Who knew?

As I have readily admitted, I know that I cannot beat the trend for new expressions. However, I do stand by my point that we must reduce our use of corporate expressions.

If all I can achieve from this book is to reduce and ridicule the use of a few expressions, that would be a step in the right direction. These are the ones I would like to eradicate.

---

16 EMEA – Europe, Middle East and Africa From experience it is very rare to find anyone who truly covers all these regions in their role so I don't know why we use it really.

Grid to play your own game of bullshit bingo (pen not included)

Pushing the envelope				
				Reach/reaching out
Open the kimono				
		End of the day		
				Blue sky thinking
			My bad	

PART 2
GLOSSARY OF EXPRESSIONS

Sesquipedalian
characterised by long words; long-winded

Floxinoxinihilipilification
The essence of nothing

I HAVE CREATED a glossary for all these expressions. Again, my thanks go to everyone who has contributed ideas and suggestions and I have incorporated as many references as I possibly could, along with some associated comments.

The main intention of the glossary is to help international businesspeople somehow start to navigate the minefield of business language. By providing a sense of what each expression means and, where possible, its source, I hope it provides a useful point of reference.

It also then gives me an outlet to make some observations and comments: some sensible, others oblique, some downright silly – this might even offer some insight into English humour and culture, if nothing else an insight into how my mind works, if you care. For me, the exercise has been enjoyable, cathartic even.

To all other readers, perhaps you would enjoy dipping in from time to time. Once I started, I couldn't stop and even as this goes to press others pop into my mind. The chances are you'll find one you use and one which the person next to you particularly likes. If I have missed one – which I am sure I have – or you hear any new ones, please do let me know. I would love to hear from you.

GLOSSARY OF EXPRESSIONS

24/7 – All the time. The / adds a bit of pizzazz, pronounce with a slur and twennyfourseven slides neatly into sentences, all the time.

80:20 rule – One of those rules which seem to apply to 80% of all situations. For example, 80% of effort is dictated by 20% of the business; 80% of all HR issues are generated by 20% of the workforce; 80% of all communication is non-verbal, which rather undermines the value of this book.

110% (giving 110%) – To put full effort into something. By giving 110% you give more than you actually have to give away which leaves the giver in deficit, which is neither good mathematics nor good short-term energy strategy.

A

A-game (bring your) – Bring your best attitude and best skills. Not to be confused with 'bringing your A-frame', which is a type of tent structure or folding ladder. That would just be odd.

Action – To do or make something – increasingly used as a verb. A European business development executive told me that a new one which he likes is "when speaking on the phone someone said 'Tell me again when I see you'. I want to see the actions when you are talking." Hmm, feels a little perverse.

Actionable – To be able to do something. This is part of the very irritating tendency to create a verb from a noun. To action something. "My biggest bugbear is the use of action as a verb. It is quite clearly a noun. I have never asked my wife if she would like me to 'action' a cup of tea for her." International publisher of Global Derivatives magazine

Activate – To start something. So if we use action as a verb, shouldn't we actionate? Not condoning, simply asking.

Actors – People. Increasingly, people talk about the key actors in business scenarios. Many of whom have massive riders, entourages and need time to find their motivation.

Actualise/Actualisation – The process of making something a reality. 'So what happened to John?' 'Actually he had actualised his dream to become an actuary.' The Oxford English Dictionary defines self-actualisation as "the realisation or fulfilment of one's talents and potentialities". So self-actualisation is the process of actually being yourself, rather than someone else. Why wouldn't you?

Advisor, trusted – The hallowed goal for any consultant. The position of trusted advisor is the pinnacle relationship with the client. Any other time, don't trust them at all.

Aligned/Alignment – Following a concept in agreement. I once heard someone once say 'we are highly aligned following the critical path'. Conjures up images of a precarious tightrope walk or star formations.

Altar, left at the – Wedding day rejection. When the other person didn't uphold their side of the agreement, not an instruction for where to sit in the church.

Anchor, lift the … and let it set sail – To start something, launch it and see whether it floats, or sinks. See also *rocket, send it up in a* and *flagpole, run it up the*.

Apples to oranges – To compare two products which are not comparable. Throughout this book I have endeavoured not to turn to Wikipedia as that would be lazy. However, I do like

GLOSSARY OF EXPRESSIONS

the international flavour it brings, not least given this book is partly aimed at international readers.

'Apples to oranges' apparently is not specific to the English language. In Quebec, Canadian French talks of 'comparer des pommes avec des oranges'; however, in European French the idiom says 'comparer des pommes et des poires (apples with pears). I wonder if there is some bitter rivalry for the supremacy of French tongue (back away from the obvious comment), perhaps better referred to as comparing apples with sour grapes.

In Latin American Spanish, it is usually 'comparar papas y boniatos', that is, to compare potatoes and sweet potatoes (potato, potarto) or 'comparar peras con manzanas' (pears and apples).

In Serbia 'Поредити бабе и жабе' compares grandmothers and toads and in Romania 'vaca și izmenele' compares a cow with longjohns and 'baba și mitraliera' compares the old lady and the machine gun, as you do. Then again, the English could be called strange for comparing chalk with cheese. They all mean the same thing, whether fruit, cow, thermal clothing, a blood relative or a rapid fire weapon.

For other fruity expressions see Pear shaped, Cherry pick, Second bite at the cherry, Pop one's cherry, Low hanging fruit.

Appraise/appraisals – To assess something or someone – a human resource process to review progress of an individual using form filling techniques. The 360 degree appraisal is a process whereby an individual is appraised by colleagues more senior, on a similar level and more junior than him or herself. Intended to seek a holistic overview of an individual. Can backfire when the sample group is too small and the recipient can attribute 'constructive' feedback – read negative comments – to an individual and hate them forever more. The process is designed as an instrument for turning around the fortunes of underperforming organisations. I heard someone refer to this process as a 360 degree transformation – so you basically turn full circle back to the point at which you started?

ASAP – Abbreviation for 'as soon as possible'. Conjures to mind smart phone applications – I want this 'ace app' but only if it is free of charge. Important to say short A not long, otherwise you end up with ArseAP, this is only acceptable if you have a South African accent, although to be honest, applicable anyone to anyone who says ASAP.

Assets – Anything making a positive contribution to an organisation such as computers, machinery – even used for employees although anyone who says 'the staff are our greatest asset' is most likely a liability. A COO of a global trading firm scoffed that someone had told him that "as a family they had decided to sell their car as it was a 'non-performing asset'..."

Sweating our assets – To make the most of something by extracting every possible value. I use it a lot in comedy I put my hand on my chest and say 'the reason I'm up here sweating my assets'. See also *Lemon, Squeezing the*.

Awesome – I have to question whether anything in the corporate world is really that awesome? Ok, maybe if it involves an amazing invention or a cure for cancer, but these should really be reserved for natural places of beauty. I mean, if an email is truly so awesome, what would you say when you see the Victoria Falls?

GLOSSARY OF EXPRESSIONS

B (beware balls, bucks and bottoms)

Back burner – Something left aside for the time being – not a sunbed or a case of not being able to reach that spot with the sun lotion. Derives from cookers – pots left on the back burner to keep warm. See also *Park an idea* and *Offline, take*.

Balls. Lots of balls in play here.

Ball, eye on the – Having a clear focus on what you are doing. Originates from a sporting references – hand-ball-eye coordination is very important in business, particularly if you're planning to smack something across the room.

Balls up – Slang for making a mess of something. Also known as a cock-up but not to be confused with an erection – 'it was a complete and total erection' does not work as a replacement unless you are describing an ugly building.

The ball is in your court – When you have made an opening bid in a negotiation, correspondence or conversation, it is the other party's turn to respond. I would have thought we would have played in the same court. Rare to see tennis played across two courts. So the ball is in on your side of the court would be fitting.

Ballparks – In the right ballpark (broadly in the right area), ballpark figures (estimates) and out of the ballpark (something done either exactly as it should be, or particularly well). Ballparks is derived from baseball. I know nothing about baseball. I have played softball, any reference to soft is a lie. Not to be confused with softplay (a squishy centre for small children).

Baseball has spawned a wide variety of weird and wonderful expressions. It would be wrong to leave them out and there are too many to include, so I have taken them offline and parked them in an Appendix.

Bandwidth – This is usually to do with a personal capacity or available time to deal with something – 'I just haven't got the bandwidth'. Nothing to do with the girth of big hairy rockers – although it might make a good name for a group: 'We are The Bandwidth, do you wanna rock?'

Bar, raise the – Derived from pole vaulting or high jumping, raising the bar essentially makes the leap more challenging. Push the bar is how you get out of a fire door. Lean on the bar is what we do after a long day.

Bark is worse than their bite – Reference from dogs, not to be confused with best of breed or dog and pony show. Usually used for posturing managers who prefer to growl than purr.

Barrel, over a – To be held under someone else's control/power and deemed helpless. Some suggest it refers to being slung over a barrel to either empty the lungs of someone saved from drowning or being given a beating/flogging. That's business for you – saved one day, whipped the next.

Barriers to entry – Reason for failure to successfully break into a market. Like driving into Canary Wharf – why do the security guards check the taxi driver by swabbing the steering wheel and the taxi, but disregard the passenger? I think passengers should be swabbed too – 'tongue out please madam, just say ah'.

Bath, take a – To suffer heavy financial losses. 'The precious metals market took a sudden tumble and as result we took a bath'. Not a reference to personal hygiene. Not to be confused with taking the plunge. This is when one commits to taking action, despite being concerned, cautious or anxious.

A slight derivation is to take an early bath, an informal British sporting reference to being sent (or dragged) off the pitch for foul (or bad) play. The player returns to the dressing room for a bath before match has finished. Generally advise against bathing references in the workplace, it doesn't feel right.

GLOSSARY OF EXPRESSIONS

Beat the street – Presumably used because it has a rhythmic lilt. The Street is a reference to Wall Street analysts' expectations for corporate earnings. Means to perform better than most, rather than perform a street dance.

Bells and whistles – With 'all the bells and whistles' – often used in technology for all the buttons and gadgets you could possibly want. A technological cacophony and where a headache is the only certainty.

Bend the rules – To accommodate or to create some leeway to help someone achieve what they want to achieve. 'In order for him to qualify, we had to bend the rules slightly'. A bent ruler, however, is an authoritative figure engaging in corrupt practices.

Best of breed – Best product on the market – apparently. This. Drives. Me. Mad. Overused. Overstated. Over it. The only thing which comes to mind when someone says best of breed is best inbred. Please stop. Note: not be confused with best in class or best in breed (classes in a pet show). While we are on the topic of animals, not to be confused with a Dog and Pony show.

Best practices – the best way to do something. If it's so good, why practice?

Big data – Masses of data –Reminds me of the 80s pop group 'Big Fun'. I think they might even have been called Big Fun! And you can't beat a good exclamation mark, like Wham! Oh I like 'Big Data!' Don't blame it on the sunshine, don't blame it on the moonlight ... blame it on the data. Don't we always? A publisher corrected me. "Big data? It should be large data!" I don't like the use of big generally – big picture, big style or signing of big kisses – it's a slippery slope to big regards, big wishes and big smackers.

While we're at it,

Big picture – Take a step back to look at the bigger picture – it is like having your picture taken where the photographer is near the edge of the cliff.

Big-ticket items – The particularly expensive elements. In a household budget these would be property, a car, yacht, villa (I can dream, can't I?). I'm not convinced by the point about the size of the ticket: a) I have never seen a ticket hanging on a house before, and b) I don't believe that they get any bigger the larger the product purchased – often they are smaller and more discrete, absent even.

Bite the bullet – To stop procrastinating, do something difficult or unpleasant, overcoming hesitation. 'In reducing headcount, she really had to bite the bullet'. Interestingly, in US slang 'Bit the big one' means that someone died. 'Did you hear that David bit the big one?'. Presumably choked on a really big bullet.

Blah, blah, blah – A cross between etcetera and 'whatever' - also expressed as yadda, yadda, yadda but not yoda, yoda, yoda or yoga, yoga, yoga.

Blamestorming – A process by which people give thought and consideration in the hope of blaming someone for the crazy idea from the blue sky thinking brainstorming session. Also known as back-peddling and arse-covering.

Blue, out of the – The opportunity to write this book came at me right out of the blue – like an unexpected bolt of lightning out of the bright blue sky.

Blue sky thinking – See Brainstorming

Boil, off the – When someone or something is not performing as well as it had previously, it is described as having gone off the boil. It might have been put on the back burner.

Boil the ocean – Used as 'you can't boil the ocean' – even if you wanted to, you couldn't reach your goal. Ridiculous expression, because it is a ridiculous goal. Why would you want to

GLOSSARY OF EXPRESSIONS

boil the ocean? Is reversing the effects of global warming a case of wanting to boil the ocean?

Boilerplate – Standardised text. Derived from rolled steel plates for making boiler heaters. A standardised approach to writing or standard pieces of text used for clauses in contracts, elements to a computer programme or standard elements (to succinctly explain a company's purpose) in a press release.

Boots on the ground – Receiving information from people qualified to talk with authority. Derives from the military; those in situ are in a better position to comment than someone far away.

Bottlenecks – Sticking points in a process. Unless you are drinking overpriced bottled water, in which case the bottle may be a perfect pyramid shape. We can learn a lot from water that has cascaded over mountains for centuries and ended up in a basement meeting room fridge just off the M25.

Bottom. Just like bucks and balls, there are many bottoms:

The bottom falls (or drops) out –A sudden collapse or failure, as in the bottom fell out of the market. if you're heavily invested, you might hit rock bottom.

Bottoms up! – Words used for a toast. Others include 'cheers!', 'down the hatch' or 'good health' which are more socially acceptable than bottoms up. Also, not to be confused with 'belly up' or 'tits up', which means that it's all gone wrong. Caution: do not raise your glass to anyone with the words 'tits up!' unless you particularly enjoy uncomfortable silences.

From the bottom up – Working on a project starting from the granular, grass roots end of the process, working one's way up to the top. 'Let's analyse this project from the bottom up'. Note distinction from bottoms up. One would not say we're working on his project from the bottoms up – it may suggest you are drinking on the job.

Get to the bottom of – To find the root cause of the problem, which at first glance might not be apparent – 'let's get to the bottom of what really went wrong' – likely involving a bottoms up approach.

To bottom out – When a situation reaches its lowest point before stabilising or improving – 'retail sales provide an indicator that the recession is at last bottoming out'. If only. Not to be confused with knock the bottom out of – the cause of creating something to collapse or falter. For example, the transport strike really knocked the bottom out of the market.

Bet your bottom dollar – An informal way to express a conviction that something is going to occur – 'you can bet your bottom dollar this will knock the bottom out of the market, best we get to the bottom of it and analyse it from the bottom up'. As you see, over-use creates an arse.

Bottom line – A point which cannot be disputed. Often interchanged with 'at the end of the day' or 'when all is said and done'. The bottom line is that it is over-used.

Box, thinking outside the – To be thinking laterally and outside the usual constraints. As a product manager of investment accounting software from Boston explains, a new derivation is "Don't just think about being inside or out – create a new box." I am so creative I've thought outside the box, decided to create a new one and I think I'll think outside that one too. I have no idea where I am.

Box, ticking all the boxes – the perfect process, product, scenario, circumstance, person – ticking all the boxes erm, well, ticks all the boxes

Brain, to pick your – To ask what you think. The editor of a hedge fund publication told me: "The most annoying phrase on the planet is 'Can I pick your brain?' Worse still is 'Can I buy you lunch and pick your brain?' One particular person caught me on a bad (deadline) day and when they refused to take no for an answer, I replied: 'If I said yes to every lunch that I was invited to, to pick my brain, I would be fat and brainless by now.' She continued 'These days I reply 'Do you subscribe, because that is where my brain is.'" A true sign of publishing times. Buying lunch and picking bread might be more appropriate.

Brainstorm – The process by which people give thought and consideration in the hope of generating a creative idea. It is worth noting that people with epilepsy don't like the expression brainstorm, so some refer to it as 'thinkshower' or 'thoughtshower'. "My absolute current favourite is 'thoughtshower'. Allied to it is 'thoughtware' which means idea/great thoughts on a subject. For example, 'Let me think about it and I'll send you some thoughtware." Senior international PR executive

Some brainstorms can be highly effective, however; I have attended some which have been less of a thinkshower, more of a cerebral dribble.

Here also must sit Blue sky thinking: a creative or visionary process to provide a framework – ideas are put forward without any constraints or parameters (such as budget, practicality or simply being judged as far-fetched).

Broken biscuits –Anything which can't be addressed or helped in a project is known as broken biscuits. In every biscuit tin there are always some broken biscuits. Does this work in the US – cracked cookies?

Breathe new life (into the project) – To inject some direction, energy and enthusiasm into a project. After all we have all sat in endless meetings wondering if the person next to us is still breathing. Anyone know CPR?

Brown bag meeting – A meeting over lunchtime to which you are expected to bring your own sandwich. It is always useful to have a brown bag at these meetings, something to breathe into when you start hyperventilating. "If you have the poor manners to pull someone into a meeting over lunchtime at least provide some lunch!" Ex-investment bank professional. Always thought it was an odd expression particularly because it started in the US. Yet in the US alcohol is hidden in brown bags – makes for a more interesting meeting perhaps?

Brownie points – Points for good deeds/achievements. Derived from the Brownie Guide movement where girls collect 'brownie points'. In my day it was a dried pea and we would collect them in special receptacle and obsessively count them out. My receptacle was a cigar tube, wouldn't be allowed now. Now it seems everyone is giving points, but no-one's collecting them – next time, ask for a dried pea or scream: Oggy, Oggy, Oggy! (History suggests this was the cry of Cornish pasty sellers letting hungry workers know that it was lunch time. Oggy is thought to derive from the Cornish 'hoggan', or pasty. Well, who knew?)

Bucks. Plenty of these in circulation.

> Here there tends to be quite a bit of confusion and it is important not to confuse the meaning or circumstance. Do not mix these up. Young bucks banging has a meaning of its own, ideally not used at the boardroom table.

To buck the trend – To go against common or crowd behaviour. For example, gold bucks the trend of depressed commodities markets.

Young buck – An old-fashioned term for a fashionable and spirited young man. Derived from a young male deer.

Buck stops here – Reaching the point of absolute and ultimate responsibility. US President Harry S Truman had a sign with this inscription on his desk.

GLOSSARY OF EXPRESSIONS

Pass the buck – To side-step or evade responsibility. It is thought to originate from poker. Back in the gunslinging second half of the 19th century, a buck was passed as a means of avoiding cheating and the inevitable shootouts if a player suspected foul play. To avoid any potential unfairness, the deal of the cards changed hands during sessions and the next in line was given a marker, often a knife, which was frequently made of the horn of a buck. When the dealer's turn was over, he would 'pass the buck'. In time, the knife was replaced by silver dollars and some suggest this could be the origin of the word 'buck' as a colloquial term for a dollar.

Bang for your buck – A buck is a colloquial term for a dollar unit of currency. Bang for the buck refers to getting a good deal for the money spent.

Big bucks – Lots of money. Big smackers also works here, weirdly, although it is worth noting that a smacker is an enthusiastic kiss, so use with caution.

Buck up – To sharpen up/become more alert. Usually used as the warning 'oh, buck up'. Don't confuse the b with an f, because that means the opposite or an incitement to fail.

Bucks fizz – a cocktail of orange juice and champagne. Also name of a 1970s group – one of UK's few winning entries for the Eurovision Song Contest, a cultural and political voting experience in itself.

Build it and they will come – This is one I hear more and more often used as a cry of confidence, which immediately suggests a lack of confidence: I'm not sure it will work and people will want it, but as a last-ditch effort to suggest that it might work, 'build it and they will come'. (Invariably it never works either.) I was told this was the cry of Gustave Eiffel in response to Parisiens' complaints about his plans to erect the Eiffel Tower, but I cannot confirm this. "If you build it he will come" is a quote from the 1989 film Field of Dreams if that helps, again much misquoted, but like me you may have lost interest now ...

Bump on a log – Someone who is deemed to be useless. To be clear, not someone who requires cosmetic assistance.

Bumpf – also known as stuff. Marketing bumpf (see also collateral), 'have you seen the bumpf about the project?'.

Bunny boiler – From the film "Fatal Attraction" with Glenn Close as the revengeful mistress. She boils Michael Douglas' child's pet rabbit. (To be clear, his character's daughter, not in real life. Catharine Zeta Jones would be furious.) In this case revenge was a dish served hot.

Burn bridges – To leave a trail of destruction behind you. Particularly used with business relationships. Important not to do this when leaving an organisation, as your colleagues (whether senior, peer group or junior) are the referees for your future. 'It seems he cannot cross a bridge without burning it behind him.'

Buy in – Agreement – to get someone's buy in. Cash need not exchange hands or any form of payment in kind, so don't be tempted or fooled.

Buzz, create some – This we get a lot; 'can you create some buzz around my product?' What? A high-pitched irritating hum that makes you think you have tinnitus?

GLOSSARY OF EXPRESSIONS

C

Cadence – A head of IT infrastructure who works a lot with Americans brought this to light. "This is an odd one but it seems to be increasingly creeping into the English language, as in 'we should set up a cadence on this one'; why not just say 'weekly meeting/conference call'? I refer to this as the 'C' word which gets people's attention." A cadence is a rhythmic flow or a sequence of sounds or words. See also singing from the same hymn sheet.

Calendarise – To make an entry in the diary. Really? Calendarise? See also diarise, along with outlookise, schedulise, notebookise and scrapofpaperise.

Captains of industry – Anyone who is a leader of an organisation, serving at the helm of their ship or anyone with an ego large enough to think they should be saluted. See also thought leaders.

Cash cow – An investment, business or product which provides a steady income or profit. Cash cows give piggy banks a run for their money.

Dairy. And while we're on a dairy train of thought (if you can have a gravy train, why not a dairy train?) there are a number of bovine by-product expressions which will crop up (farming pun intended) in everyday conversation:

Cream:

Cream of the crop – Of best possible calibre.
  Cream always rises to the top, but so does the grand fromage (see big cheese), and how many grand fromages are the cream of the crop is often debatable, also a rule of diminishing rechurns (sorry).

Creaming it in – Doing very well financially out of something, presumably the cash cow.

The cat that's got the cream – Feeling very pleased with oneself ... dealing with a group of people who have performed a great achievement herding cats that have got the cream.

Butter:

It's the bread and butter of the business – The day-to-day source of income for the business to keep it ticking over and without which it may not be able to continue.

Bread always falls on the buttered side – If something goes wrong, it really goes wrong. You can pick up again, but it's going to be unappetising.

Bread-and-butter letter – A letter or note of thanks or acknowledgement after an event, follow-up notes.

Butter someone up – To flatter them in the hope of receiving something favourable in return, can be a benefit of a well written bread-and-butter letter.

Butter wouldn't melt (in someone's mouth) – Reference to someone who is acting as if they are innocent when they evidently are not.

Fine words butter no parsnips – Words come easily, but actions speak louder than words.

Know which side your bread is buttered on – Other than it's the side which will hit the floor when you drop the bread, it means to know where your income comes from, it may be from having buttered someone up with a bread-and-butter letter.

Milk:

No use crying over spilled milk – No point being unhappy about something you cannot rectify. Don't waste time crying, get mopping before it turns sour.

GLOSSARY OF EXPRESSIONS

To milk someone or something – To exploit something, or elicit information or a favourable reaction from an audience. The key is to know when to stop before it turns sour.

Milk of human kindness – Care and compassion for others. From Macbeth by William Shakespeare: "Yet doe I feare thy Nature, It is too full o' th' Milke of humane kindnesse."

The land of milk and honey – A biblical reference to an imaginary place where the pickings are plentiful, the grass is always greener on the other side – looking to a land of milk and honey.

Cheese:

Hard cheese – A convivial and informal expression which is used either to empathise over a small matter, or to show that you have no sympathy for them (the question is, how do you tell the difference and it can't be from an exclamation mark). In Australia apprently they say ' Stiff cheese!'

Say cheese – A method used by photographer to encourage the person to smile. From experience it works in English (cheese) German (Käse) but not so well in French (fromage).

Big cheese – The most important person, also known as the 'grand fromage'. Today the big cheese can often be used with a slightly derogatory connotation. I prefer to think of myself as a big chalk.

Cheesed off – To be disgruntled or angry with someone or something. Often the big cheese.

Cheese someone off – To irritate or make someone else disgruntled or angry with you.

Cut the cheese – To release intestinal gas. Apparently, this is also known as cut the mustard, but I had never heard this before. I always thought that if you cut the mustard it meant you meet the grade and suit very well.

> **Chalk and cheese, to be like** – To be different from each other. See also apples and oranges.

Cash injection – An investment or pay rise, could also be a shot in the arm.

Catalyst – Some say catalyst, others say agents of change or change agents – whatever they're called, it's like herding catalysts – you direction changers, you.

Cats, herding – One of my favourites, right up there with throwing my toys out of the pram. Working with senior executives and entrepreneurs I am often found herding catalysts.

CC – To copy you in – 'I'll cc you'. CC is derived from a time (not so long, scarily) ago when we used to type everything in triplicate using carbon paper. The person receiving a copy, received a 'carbon copy'. To notify that it was a copy, we would type 'cc Jane Smith'. If someone was blind carbon copied, i.e. bcc, it would be overtyped onto their copy alone as bcc Jane Smith. This was back in the day before the internet was invented. (Now I feel old.) This was back in the day before the internet was invented.

Centric – At the heart of: customer-centric, employee-centric, call-centric.

Change managers / agents of change / change agents – People in organisations whose role is specifically to get people to do things differently. Usually lovers of thinking outside the box, blue sky thinking and brainstorming. Full of thoughtware and if male, probably jiggles his change.

Characterise – To explain something. Let me explain this to you but first I must do a vocal and physical warm-up then find my motivation.

GLOSSARY OF EXPRESSIONS

Charm offensive – To go out with the intention of being nice. On paper an oxmoryon, in reality likely a moron – why not be pleasant all the time? People will be less suspicious.

Chemistry session – First impression relationship testing session. 'Before we commit to working together we should have a chemistry session.' Maybe we should say 'let's light the bunsen burners and melt the biros'.

Cherry pick – To pick with great care and only the best. May not be low hanging fruit.

Cherry, get a second bite at the – To get a second attempt at trying something. Presumably your own cherry, don't try to bite someone else's, that would be rude.

Cherry, pop one's – To lose one's virginity – sounds careless now I read it back. Note difference from cloggs, pop one's. Two things in life you won't experience twice.

Circle back – Getting back to someone, presumably without any points. Makes me think of barn dancing, 'circle back and dosey doe your partner.' See also revert.

Circle, square the – No idea. Make something complete? Invented by someone who wasn't very good at putting the round peg in the round hole in kindergarten. "Square the circle? WTF does that mean???!" Investment banking professional.

Clogs, pop one's – To die, also known as passing away or on. You see my point about not confusing with pop one's cherry – when referring to the passing of Great Aunt Joan, although it might lighten the mood.

Collateral - another name for the description of leaflets, brochures, fact sheets etc. (See also bumpf.) If it gets battered in a brief case or in transit to a conference, it becomes collateral damage. Also a financial requirement for money put up front to cover the cost of something: collateral to cover an exposure. Which is why it is always useful to take a brochure to your conference hotel should you get locked out of your room naked without a towel. In which case your first question must be 'does my bumpf look big in this?'

Comfort break – To take a formal break in proceedings to go the lavatory. I have also heard it called a 'bio-break' and I wondered whether we were taking time out to recycle? In truth I don't mind 'comfort breaks', it is the most diplomatic way of getting around, lavatory vs. loo vs. toilet (yes, I can feel your judgement) vs. bathroom vs. restroom. So shouldn't we then call it the comfort room? I guess it depends on the fluffiness of the towels. Bio-break should be discouraged. As should bladder-break, in case you were tempted. Note important difference from comfort zone.

Comfort zone – Doing tasks and being in environments where we are most comfortable – mine's on the sofa with a good film.

Core competencies – One's fundamental attributes, nothing to do with abdominals. Not that I would know: as far as I am concerned, in that area it's more a case of core incompetencies. Also known as core capabilities. My core is definitely incapable.

Counter – We are all countering these days: counterparty, counterproductive, counterintuitive, over the counter, under the counter, brief encounter. I have always thought that counteractive should mean lazy.

Critical – Everything is bloody critical – or should that be bleeding critical? Critical success factors, critical alignment, critical thinking, critical paths, critical feedback, critical cycles. I hate to critique creatures of critical communications and I do appreciate that it also means analytical but I can't help ask, is it really as critical as all that? Heart surgery is a critical service, but it's still not rocket science.

GLOSSARY OF EXPRESSIONS

Critical mass – The ideal amount for something to start being successful. This derives from physics, namely the minimum amount of fissile material needed to maintain a nuclear chain reaction. Nothing to do with sceptical Catholic worship.

Crowdsourcing – Research – when we ask other people for thoughts and contributions. Age old concept, new name.

Crystal ball – To tell the future or estimate it at least. Should it become 'crystamate'? (Not to be confused with crystal meth – some may claim this tells a bright future, but too much and one thing is predetermined – it will turn ugly.)

Customer-facing – Description of a role where an individual deals with customers. The rest of us keep our backs firmly turned.

Cut to the chase – To get to the interesting point/insightful moment. It is believed to originate from the silent film industry. Many scenes featured romantic moments followed by action-packed chase sequences and was used as script direction: 'Jannings escapes... Cut to chase.' Used today as an alternative to 'to get to the point' or 'to cut a long story short', inevitably followed by a long rambling explanation.

Cut and thrust – An expression of enthusiasm. Derives from hand-to-hand combat, mostly used in the context of competitive business or a fundamental point to an argument. No blood should be shed, unless from an accidental paper cut.

Cutting edges – One of my favourite lines from the song 'Bullshit Bingo' is 'the edges they are leading, they're cutting and we're bleeding'. We talk about the 'leading edge of technology' which became the 'cutting edge' of technology and on further improvement became 'bleeding edge'. Have we reached the bleeding brink?

Cylinders, firing on all – When everything involved is working at their best possible performance – like a highly performant car.

D

Darwinian, it's – Presumably this has something to do with the survival of the fittest. This would be a great new work-out class: Join our new class every Tuesday at noon: 'Darwinian fitness'. To quote Darwin: "Fitness is often defined as a propensity or probability, rather than the actual number of offspring." According to Maynard Smith, British evolutionary biologist, "Fitness is a property, not of an individual, but of a class of individuals." A bit like Zumba?

There are two commonly used measures of fitness: absolute fitness and relative fitness. Welcome to the 'relative fitness class' – also known as bring your family to the gym day. How fit is your family? Bring along a relative and train together – how do you compare? I'd definitely bring an aged aunt. Would make me look positively athletic.

Day, at the end of – Ranked second most irritating on the 'Lingua Franca Podium of Iritation'. Used as a replacement for 'after all' or 'in conclusion' or 'taking everything into account' but has even progressed to being used as an 'infiller' – a bit like 'like' or 'd'ya know what I mean?'. Simply, at the end of the day we all go home.

In business, people talk about 'close of play' or 'close of business' as deadlines. These are abbreviated as cop or cob which should not be confused with police or corn. Presumably close of play was created by kindergarten teachers, with remarkable application to business – screaming, shouting, throwing toys out of pram etc. It does beg the question, in a global world of virtual working, mobile technology and social media, when is the end of the day? At the log off, I suppose.

Decimate – Frequently misused in the sense of destroy, or remove a large percentage of something. A senior advisor and a highly regarded investment management CIO set the record straight: "It is often referred to in terms of 'severely reduced' when it should be 'reduced by a tenth.'"

GLOSSARY OF EXPRESSIONS

Deep dive – To look into something in great detail. I think we should start a new one: 'take a wet suit approach to the problem'. On second thought, let's not.

Deliverables – A deliverable is an element of a project; a task. Right up there with an actionable. Before dinner I thought I'd have a drinkable before ordering an edible, a demonstrable illustrating an unbelievable.

Devil is in the detail – Looking into the detail will uncover any important potential issues or obstacles. A drill down, deep dive or drains up investigation only reveals devils.

Diarise – See calendarise.

Demonstrably – To make sure that progress has some evidence to support it. Tends to be over-used, and is fast becoming like 'I literally died last week'.

Dogs. There are lots of dog references.

Why have a dog and bark yourself? – Why hire someone else to do the job and do the job yourself? An alternative is 'why buy a dog and wag the tail ourselves?' Well, quite.

Dog eat dog – A highly competitive environment. In the City I refer to this as 'dog eat sushi'.

Top dog – A dominant person in a situation or hierarchy. It is interesting to note that we haven't adopted überdogs, only überbitches.

Underdog – The competitor least likely to win a fight or context, or a person facing adversity or in a position of inferiority. Shouldn't this be unterdog? On a cultural note, as Brits we tend to favour the underdog.

Dog and pony show – A term used to explain an elaborately staged activity, performance, presentation or event designed to convince the audience for political or commercial means.

A colloquial term thought to originate in the US from the late 19th and early 20th centuries, A dog and pony show is a small travelling circus derived from the common use of performing dogs and ponies as the main attractions. Commonly it is used as a term of derision to express disdain and mistrust.

Imagine queuing outside a bar or nightclub in the cold and wet. Your entry is prevented by a velvet rope at the knee level of two huge bouncers sporting clipboards with a long magical list on which your name does not appear. An hour passes and you are desperate for a comfort break. When you are finally allowed in and have been charged an insane amount for the privilege, the club is only about quarter full. That is a dog and pony show.

Eat our own dog food – also known as 'dogfooding', a means for a company to illustrate confidence in its own products. Derived from a 1980s Canadian television advertisement for a brand of dog food in which the presenter claimed to feed the brand to his own dogs. Another possible source refers to the president of Kal Kan Pet Food, said to have eaten a can of his dog food at shareholders' meetings – a precursor to today's brand of AGM humble pie perhaps?

This was then allegedly adopted in 1988, when one Microsoft manager sent a member of the testing team an email entitled 'Eating our own Dogfood', challenging him to increase internal usage of the company's product.

Run with the big dogs – Apparently if you want to run with the big dogs, you have to pee in the tall grass or stop peeing like a puppy. Right, I'll bear that in mind.

I was wondering where to mention this, and here seems to be as good a place as any. Over the past six months I have been talking to many people and one expression I had not heard before came to light: It means essentially you can't fix

> everything so you have got to kill some puppies along the way. Oh, where to start? I asked whether the puppies had big eyes and floppy ears and was told to get a grip, breed doesn't matter – so at least it is indiscriminate.

Dodger – A slang expression for someone who is avoiding something – coffin dodger (old person), soap dodger (smelly person), tax dodger (aka jammy dodger).

Dot the i's and cross the t's – To get everything in final order, parlicularly the details.

Double digit – Used as an expression for 10-20 per cent growth but I hold two fingers up to that – it means that the business has grown more than 9.99 and less than 99 per cent.

Double-click – "We should double-click on this one" (we should explore sub groups or more detail) Head of Financial Services, EMEA for an IT Infrastructure firm. To open up As in 'double-click that idea'. To open up or look into something in greater detail. We should never talk about double-clicking unless popping back a dislocated shoulder.

Double dip – Particularly timely as I write, as we seem to be dipping a toe into the second dip of recession, although it is not clear whether or not we really are in recession again. We must stop dunking our crisps in a sauce, taking a bite and then returning for a second dunk – unless it is taramasalata, in which case you can keep it to yourself and fill your crisps.

Downsizing – To lay people off. A Communication Director of city firms explains, "'downsize' = fired / lay-off = fired / time off with your family = fired / for personal reasons = fired / CV consultancy = fired." See also leaving to pursue other interests, spend more time with his/her family, rightsizing, redundancy.

Drains up - to examine something from the bottom up. It's going to be a messy exercise.

Dream on – To dismiss something as a silly idea. 'Yeah right, dream on.' I can see it being used to explain dozing off in conferences and meetings – 'I was just dreaming on the idea.' Dream on, doze off. Conference kid.

Drill down – To look into something in detail. See also deep dive.

Ducks in a row, get your – To ensure the small details or elements are accounted for and in their proper positions. There are some expressions which, when you say them, I will struggle to hear what you say next. This is one, alongside reach out. I will have an urge to quack – perhaps in my head, perhaps aloud, but it will be there and I likely will miss your point. Ducks and office desks don't go together.

A telecoms business development manager is right there with me. "My all-time devil child (that could that be one as well!) is 'let's get our ducks in a row'. Aaarrrgghhhh! I do not personally own any ducks and why does anyone think getting ducks in a row is a good thing – is it even possible, looking at the ducks on my local pond?"

If I have to explain why this is ridiculous for duck's sake, I shall. Firstly, there is the impossibility of lining up ducks – really, it will never be perfect, just like herding catalysts. If you are always striving for perfect alignment, you will be disappointed. Why not be satisfied with getting your ducks facing in similar direction (point them towards the pond), but don't expect them to stand in formation. Some believe this refers to mother ducks trying to persuade their offspring to paddle along in formation. But then shouldn't it be ducklings in a row?

If nature must provide a guide, then I like the notion of migration formation flying. The most efficient arrangement is a V-formation behind the leader, which allows each duck to take advantage of reduced wind resistance. Having all of one's metaphorical ducks in a row would be just as efficient and logical as flying in such an organised formation.

Some suggest this may originate from shooting them ... but not when they're waddling away with their backs towards you, that's just cowardly ... oh I've just ruined it now, cute little ducks blown out of the water (with a bazooka, obviously). This is no better than kill some puppies and hope they meant fairground duck formation.

The most plausible source I can find derives from bowling. The early bowling pins were supposedly shorter and thicker than modern pins, which led to the nickname 'ducks'. Before the advent of automatic resetting machines, these 'duck pins' would be manually replaced between bowling rounds. Having one's ducks in a row would be a metaphor for having all of the bowling pins organised and properly placed before sending the next ball down the lane. I like this; however, the argument slightly falls down (pun intended) because our ducks are supposed to be in a row. Unless it is a row – as in argument – in which case, the argument stands up (pun intended) because they all crowd around a central pin (in a confrontational, almost bullying formation?). This has only made my position worse: no longer will I be quacking, but instead wondering about the argumentative pins.

E

Eating our lunch – Having one's business eroded by a competitor. When I was seven my mother was sent home a letter requesting she give me more in my packed lunch as I was eating other people's. (I will ... regret sharing that.) I have also heard 'stealing sandwiches from our lunchbox'.

Edge – To be at the forefront of something, used with cutting, leading and bleeding. Bleeding is thought to be edge of all edges.

> **Eggs.** A few cracking phrases.
>
> You've got to break an egg to make an omelette. This is advisable, although some people don't like the idea and must have to be convinced. How do they make omelette? Please don't say packet mix.
>
> **Over egging the cake, or overegging the pudding** (or is it dessert? Never sweet.) – To overdo something, take it a little too far. As one who can't stomach anything gelatinous/pudding'y, the thought of an egg-based pudding is sickening – other than a crème brulée, which is always acceptable, oh and a good tiramisu ... or profiterole ... I'm afraid that my argument is fast disappearing, a bit like the crème brulée.

Elephant in the room – The difficult subject which people cannot ignore. It seems we have moved on from ignoring the elephant in the corner, it has grown in confidence and stepped out from the shadows. Now we must eat the elephant.

As a network communications specialist put it to me: "Julia, the only way to eat an elephant is in bite size chunks." A senior strategist went further: "Which is presumably poached as we boil the ocean. Eating the whole elephant, in the room, presumably in the corner?"

GLOSSARY OF EXPRESSIONS

Embracing the idea – Taking an idea into consideration. G'waan, put your arms around it and give it a cuddle.

Engine room – Usually used by managers who think they are being complimentary, but in actual fact patronising. In guiding a client or new employee through an office they remark in a slightly raised voice, "so this is the engine room" (greasy, oily, messy – actually they may have a point). See also powerhouse.

Enjoy! – Used by waiting staff as food is served. A senior fund management journalist said: "Enjoy! Is my hate after being served. Suppose I don't want to? Suppose I fail to? Quite an expectation to live up to."

Enterprise – It was a buzzword of the late 90s /early 2000s when everyone talked about enterprise. Not as in entrepreneurism, but computer and systems networking across an organisation.

Envelope, push the – To push the boundaries. Nothing to do with making a cash-in-envelope act of bribery. Also heard as 'stretch' the envelope. I have never understood this, why does moving stationery make you achieve more?

Escalate – To take an issue to a higher authority. Escalate vs. escapade vs escalope (perhaps a secret office affair with someone more senior, resulting in marriage).

Expectation management – Best to manage the expectations of the client/your boss. Usually that they think you're going to do a good job. What a thought – best set them straight immediately.

Exposure – Used a great deal in PR, advertising and marketing – all about getting the client exposure. But there is such a thing as over-exposure. It's not decent.

F

Face time – Spending time face-to-face. Also known as 'pressing flesh'. In an increasingly virtual world there is an argument for more time spent in person, but 'face time'? Why not 'body time'? Perhaps we should call videoconferencing 'virtual visaging' (for best effect use French accent), visage time or countenance calls?

Facilitation (facilitator) – Managing/guiding the process. Someone who likes flipcharts, whiteboards, marker pens and parking ideas by taking them offline.

Failure is not an option – Er, it is. Always is.

To be fair – A declaration of one's effort to be reasonable, which suggests that it is the other party who should be reasonable, most likely followed by an insult.

Family, spending time with – Fired. Often used in employee communications after someone has left the organisation. See also pursue other interests, downsizing, rightsizing and redundancy.

Fast track – Accelerated programme of achievement, particularly for those singled out as high performers. Also a quicker route through airport security.

Feeding frenzy – Launching a product which creates huge demand – like the strangely sudden interest in fish spa pedicures, mostly conducted in a shop window – why is that?

Fish out of water – Uncomfortable feeling of being in the wrong environment. Like sitting in a shop window with your feet in a fish tank.

Gone fishing – Possibly a form of denial that you're sitting in a shop window with your feet in a fish tank. Gone pfishing means they're trying to hack your account.

Fit for purpose – Good enough for the job for which it was intended. If we focus too much on the word 'fit', most of us

GLOSSARY OF EXPRESSIONS

would never be able to do the job for which we were intended. Should be a name for a City gym. Tends to be used in the negative – not fit for purpose.

Flagpole, run it up and see if it flies – To see if it works. An expression over-used in my early career of idiom abuse.

See also anchor, lift the and rocket, send it up in a

Food for thought – Makes you think hard about something, probably the next meal.

Fork – As in 'stick a fork in it'. To see if it is ready. Like checking sausages on a barbecue. 'Let's see if there's salmonella in this sausage' would be a great expression.

Foot in the door – Make the first step. Stems from a house-to-house sales person's approach – once you have a foot in the door, it cannot be closed on you.

Footprints – One's impact or trail behind you. Mostly used in the sense of carbon usage and environmental footprint, more recently extended to technology footprints and contributions to projects. We fight to reduce them. When they disappear entirely, worry.

Frothy (it's looking) – Looking good. Like a beautifully poured skinny soya double shot cappuccino. I have no idea if that is correct, I drink mine black.

Fruit, low-hanging – A target that can be easily reached, or a goal that can be accomplished with little effort – projects should come to low hanging fruition.

Fruition – To bear fruit. Pronounced frooo-ition – not fruitshun (one who avoids their five a day).

Small fry – Something considered to be insignificant or unimportant. The exact opposite of the British legend Stephen Fry.

Fudge factor – An element built into a project to allow for post-result massaging to ensure that the results fit the expectations – manipulation, basically.

Full English breakfast – A pronouncement of full commitment. As a head of policy of a government agency put it me: "The chicken's involved and the pig's committed". See also skin in the game – presumably a sausage skin connection.

Future proofing – A suggestion that a product of service will still work in the future and/or protect the customer from anything which will happen in the future – a field force for future generations to come?

A journalist said: "I mean, just what the hell is that? You waterproof tangible stuff, like a roof or a basement. How do you proof against something intangible?

G

Game face – Visually preparing yourself for a battle. Er, also known as a meeting with biscuits. Armour and chain mail are not required.

Game changer – Something which will significantly affect the course or planning of events. Is this something to do with a gaming console? I do find it very hard to change games without calling on a small child.

Game plan – Also just a plan. But we feel either more military or more nerdy talking about game plans. I've seen quite a few game over plans.

Gate, out of the – Right from the start. Originates from horse racing – the gates open to ensure that the horses have a fair chance of starting at the same time from the same point.

Kicking it up a gear – Move it up a level. A bit like raise the metabolic rate, and make a step change. Also shifting gears, but what if I only drive an automatic?

Get your head around it – To consider and understand a concept. Similar to embrace an idea, we basically give it a cuddle. Does not apply to all body parts. Don't wrap your legs around an idea – this is not to be explored anywhere near a boardroom table, although some may have tried.

Glue – The person who holds or pulls (sometimes drags) an organisation together. Usually the person who organises the social drinks.

Goal posts – What we are aiming to achieve. They never stay still.

Go no go – As in 'what's our go no go plan?' What's going to determine whether the plan goes ahead or not. This should never be written down – too many o's looks suspicious or like an island in the Indian ocean…..this year I shall be taking a holiday on the remote island of Gonogo.

Go to market – Launch a product. Always makes me think of 'this little piggy' from the children's rhyme. This little piggy went to market. This little piggy stayed in his cubicle. This little piggy had pastrami on rye and this little piggy was on a diet. And this little piggy went weeeeee all the way home on a 'Boris bike' (the colloquial name for a London rental bike).

Go-to person – Point of (informed) contact. Rather than a back away person – we all know who they are.

Going forward – Henceforth, from here on in. As a journalist commented, "'We'll be doing X going forward'. As opposed to what? Going back? Have you invented time travel?"

But what to use instead? Heed the advice of Lucy Kellaway. In her Financial Times column of 4 November 2007, she quoted a report by the Federal Reserve stating: "Increased uncertainty has the potential to restrain economic growth going forward." She insists that "The last two words could and should be simply crossed out." She continues, "If, on occasion, there is a need to spell out the idea of the future, we have some perfectly good words already. For pompous people there is 'henceforth' and, for the rest of us, there is 'in the future.'"

Other derivations are creeping in, such as 'working on a go forward basis'. 'Go forward strategies' –that's not a strategy. Clocks tick, time passes, we do things.

Going gangbusters – To do something with great energy and enthusiasm. If something is going well it may be referred to as 'going gangbusters' (e.g. the market was going gangbusters for telecom stocks). Also referred to as going great guns or doing something with great gusto. A journalist added, 'Not to be confused with going 'Ghostbusters', too much fun for business life.'

Granularity – The finer details – look at the 'granularity of the problem'. A financial services salesperson highlighted this

GLOSSARY OF EXPRESSIONS

'Granularity' – took me a long time to work out what they were using it for and now occasionally only just manage to stop myself falling into the trap. So why not granulated, casterised or looking at a problem from an icing sugar perspective?

Grenade, throw in a – To contribute disruptively to events or discussions. Can be a positive contribution to challenge an idea. Particularly annoying when a suited adult enacts pulling the pin with their teeth, throwing and ducking. Worse still, says, 'wait for it', then five seconds later, 'boom'.

Grass roots – Take it back to grass roots level – back to basics. Some roots can strangle, so be careful what you wish for. A marketing manager wrote, "I hate marketing jargon … 'let's take it back to grass roots level' – why not just say it as it is?"

Greasy pole – Career progression in the corporate world. In 1868 on his appointment as Prime Minister Benjamin Disraeli is quoted as saying, "I have climbed to the top of the greasy pole." Still applies today. Picture your career progression as trying to climb a fireman's pole (or for male readers a pole dance pole, if that helps – oh, I may have lost you …) and it is covered in moisturiser (and why not? We do live in the metrosexual age of male grooming).

Growth – Improvement in the condition of a business. Not to be confused with a wart or 'boil', in turn not to be confused in context of 'boil the ocean'.

Increasingly used with 'negative'. A commercial director of a publishing house ranted: "Negative growth – do you mean shrinkage? Because either it gets bigger or it gets smaller; it does not get negatively bigger."

Guestimation – An approximation, first used by my boss at the accountancy firm who was a 'banker'. I think 'estiguess' sounds better. 'At my best estiguess' and if I'm feeling controversial, 'this is my best edgiguess'.

H

Hand over fist – To be out of control. Usually used in 'losing money hand over fist'. Not a cover up or variation on the game of rock paper scissors?

Handle – As in 'to get a handle on something'. To fully understand something. Also to 'get to grips with something' and that's not someone's throat.

Hard stop – The time at which a meeting or call must finish. People usually have to say 'I have a hard stop at 10.30' because other people find it hard to stop.

Hard truths – Harsh reality. Suggests that for some being truthful is hard. A publisher told me, "Truth is neither hard nor soft. Truth has no texture at all. They may be difficult to confront or accept but they are not hard."

Another journalist added, "Aren't all truths quite hard? A bit like, 'you've put on weight'? "

Hat – As in 'putting my xx hat on'. Speaking or acting in a certain capacity. As in 'putting my health and safety hat on' (although technically, that should be). When people say this, the Tom Jones' rendition of 'You can leave your hat on' from the film The Full Monty plays in my head. The mix of stripping and meetings can be very disturbing.

Hats, wearing many– Having many different roles and responsibilities. Like a dressing-up box.

Heads up – To let someone know in advance; to give them a heads up. There are a number of theories about the origin of the expression, ranging from a form of baseball called 'heads up baseball' and the concept of confident play; a display screen used on aircraft called a 'heads up' display; and to be given an instruction to keep your 'heads up' and become alert. Just wanted to give you a heads up that I'm calling heads before I head to the head. 'The head' is an entirely different meaning here.

GLOSSARY OF EXPRESSIONS

The head is the bathroom on a ship, which leads to another subset: nautical expressions. A few include:

Chewing the fat – To talk something over. Originates from the 19th century staple diet of salted beef. Suitable for long voyages the beef had to be chewed for hours to make it edible.

Between the devil and the deep – Used as 'caught between the devil and the deep blue sea'. To be caught in an awkward position. The 'devil' seam on wooden ships ran from bow to stern. When at sea, the devil had to be caulked (a process to seal the joints) and a sailor was suspended precariously over the side in a bo'sun's chair, often when the ship was under full sail.

Devil to pay – Describes an unpleasant result from an action. On board, caulking the 'devil' – see above – was deeply disliked and was the punishment for wrongdoing.

Know the ropes – To know what one is doing. When written on a novice seaman's discharge notice, to indicate that all the sailor knew were names and uses of the main ropes. Today used in the opposite sense – to know the ropes is a reference to knowing what you are doing – a positive rather than a limitation. Presumably show someone the ropes – to teach them the basics – comes from a similar heritage.

Headset – Similar to mindset, state of mind or 'what I think' – to my mindset we should get a headset. Noise reduction would be best.

Headspace, taking up – Taking up part of the brain – generally too much, like this definition. 'I need some headspace' means I need some space/time to think.

Hearts and minds – Businesses are all about winning hearts and minds. I don't want people to fall in love with me, nor to brainwash them.

Helicopter views – High level strategic view of a project and or process from a very expensive piece of tin powered by two blades.

I hear you – Means I don't. Simply, I disagree with you, but I'm going to waste a bit of time first. See also taking on board.

Heavy lifting – Dealing with the tough stuff, usually on behalf of someone else. Sounds macho, but let's face it, we don't lift anything heavy in these days of light laptops and lite software.

Hindsight, benefit of – History has shown, on reflection, we're all wise after the event. The good thing is I can't see my hind.

High level – Important or strategic. Although a London editor told me, "High level to mean 'general' is the most annoying."

Hit the ground running – To get started with great energy. If you are jumping into a project it is best you get your legs moving before you start, an action similar to treading water, although that has a different connotation. Does not mean that as you run you should squat down and thump the earth. Would be an interesting alternative athletic event – the opposite of hurdles.

Whole hog – The whole way. 'We went the whole hog' – particularly on a hog roast, I could go a whole hog on a hog roast.

Honest – To be very honest, to be honest with you – also means I'm about to disagree with you, or worse, insult you. A former investment banking professional told me, "I am instantly suspicious of people who regularly feel the need to preface statements 'to be honest with you' …."

Around the Horn – The longwinded way to do or say something. Derives from having to sail around the Horn of Africa as the only route between Europe and the East Indies before the Suez Canal was carved. Nothing to do with being sexually aroused, unless diatribe turns you on.

GLOSSARY OF EXPRESSIONS

Horses. Plenty of these to back.

Flogging a dead horse – Trying to sell something no-one wishes to buy.

Horses for courses – Different people like and are adept at different things. Not a reference to food.

Putting the cart before the horse – Doing something in the wrong order. Like putting in tonic before the gin.

Human capital – Simply, employees. Often used as 'human capital is our greatest asset', or more recently, I have heard employees referred to as human collateral, which only makes me think of collateral damage (nothing to do with brochures although I have heard someone say that the staff are our walking advertisements).

Hygienic – Apparently used by a firm as a description for the optimal amount of working capital on an organisation's balance sheet. Rightly ridiculed by FT columnist Lucy Kellaway.

I

Incentivise – To bribe someone to do something, but in a socially more acceptable way.

Injection – Addition. Usually used as injection of cash or injection of life. See also shot in the arm.

Insights – Sharing insights, as opposed to outsights, roundsights and undersights – but we do have oversights, and if it's a major oversight, presumably it is an übersight?

Intelligence – In addition to being a gauge of our intellect, this is often used as a meaning for information. Used by people who labour under a strange pretence that they could be secret agents as they endeavour to reach for their third chocolate biscuit undetected.

J

> **Jam.** Can be a sticky area.
>
> **Money for jam** – Easy money. See money for old rope.
>
> **You want jam on it** – You expect too much. If you want jam and peanut butter, you're taking liberties.
>
> **Jam today, jam tomorrow** – Jam tomorrow means something pleasant you wish to occur in the future but likely never will. Choose marmalade instead.

Joker, play the – Two meanings: either to play your trump card, the card with greatest value which beats all other cards, or to play the fool. Both meanings apply when it's all to play for.

Join the dots – Complete the picture. Join the dots, or dot-to-dot is designed to help children learn to draw. Other children's games useful for business include sleeping lions (most successful during the first conference session after lunch), pass the parcel (pass the biscuits while someone is speaking, only when they stop can you take one and you have to eat it before someone else speaks) and musical chairs. I believe there is a direct correlation between number of chairs and time spent in meetings. When the music stops we can sit down and do some work.

K

Key learnings – The main points we have learned from an activity or project. Mine start with trying to remember where I put them.

Kick(ing) off – Can't beat a good kick off. It means either to lose one's cool (he's kicked off), a first meeting on a project (kick off meeting) or a first thought (here's an idea for a kick off). Here's an idea for kick off, let's bet he'll kick off about the importance of a kick off.

Open the kimono – A moment in a negotiation at which a party reveals information, presumably about their sweet spot. Misunderstood because to open a kimono is made up of metres of material. Opening a kimono would take a long, long time.

Knowledge transference – We impart knowledge and intelligence rather than good old-fashioned information. Knowledge transference basically means that I'll let you know something and then perhaps you could let me know something back? It's good to share.

Knowledge management – A way of retaining the information that someone has just 'transferred' – it's more than just talking and sharing, we need to remember it too. Or as financial journalist explained: "Knowledge management is a system for retaining information held in the heads of your middle management, so you can 'rationalise' them without having to hire them back as management consultants in six months."

Drink the Kool Aid – I must confess that I had no idea what this meant. I thought it might be a post-exercise isotonic drink. I also wasn't sure whether this was Kool Aid, Cool Ade or Cool aid, a St Johns Ambulance volunteer with a bit of a swagger. Winner of Forbes Magazine's list of 'The Most Annoying, Pretentious and Useless Business Jargon' as voted by readers in 2012.

In North America 'drinking the Kool Aid' refers to the unquestioning belief of an individual or group. It carries a sinister tone from its derivation from the Jonestown Massacre of November 1978. Members of 'the people's temple' were said to have committed group suicide by drinking 'Flavor Aide' – so not actually Kool Aid – which was laced with cyanide. Some argue that they were forced to drink, rather than doing so willingly, and some stories tell that Reverend Jim Jones had on previous occasions run rehearsals with uncontaminated drinks, leading some members to believe that on the day, the drink was harmless.

What's in your water cooler?

L

Leading edges – An expression for the best that technology could possibly be, for now. In nautical terms, the leading edge is the edge of a sail that faces the wind or is the front edge of the wing or propeller of an aeroplane. Apparently, it is also a pulse signal with an increasing modifier leading-edge. (Well, quite.) My fear for leading edge is that it is close to, well, the edge, of further evolution and must caution that it never be used in the form of an 'edge leader' unless you are a lemming.

Leading provider of – Pretty much every journalist I wrote to came back with a hatred for this one. As one put it to me: "Leading? By whose measure?" Another said, "Everything is the leading software provider or leading broker-dealer or leading consultancy. Some of the firms that make this claim are tiny ones that you've never heard of, proving that 'leading' is absolutely meaningless." Well, that couldn't be clearer.

Learning curves – As in 'I'm on a steep learning curve'. This means please ignore all my questions and thoughts until I really know what I'm talking about. When you hear 'learning curve', by the time you've counted to 10, I'll bet you hear them say 'deep dive'.

At the end of July, I received an email suggesting that my business could get ahead of the holiday curve. Ugh. Really?! You really know how to do that?

Learnings – Points and actions, action points arising, also known as a takeaways (curry, every time). It's not about points any more. It's about what we've taken away to build on – we even call them key learnings. Throughout the month we leak earnings.

Lemon, squeezing the – Extracting very last possible ounce of value out of something, often extracting every possible ounce of value to the extent it may turn sour. See also sweating assets.

Level, take it to the next – Progressing to a further stage. Business is just like computer games. Behind those mystical boardroom doors you get magic powers, sometimes in the form of fruit. See also kicking up a gear.

GLOSSARY OF EXPRESSIONS

Leverage – To take advantage of something to a gain a further benefit. There are only two acceptable uses of 'leverage': 1) if you are a physicist and are actually interested in levers; and 2) if I was the global head of purchasing at global conglomerate Unilever, in which case you wouldn't be able to shut me up about my 'Unileverage'.

As an account director of an international financial services company based in Moscow told me, "I hate, I loathe 'leverage' instead of 'use.'"

Liaising – This makes me very cross and I explain in the first half of this book, I banned my team from using it. To their credit they could spell it, and the way to remember how is that liaise has two i's, as does irritate.

Lifeblood – A patronising way of saying we couldn't do without someone without using the words 'couldn't do without' because they'll demand a pay rise. See also glue, engine room and powerhouse.

Lite – This is a less than full version of a software project, usually given free of charge or at a discount so that you need a full upgrade in order to take on the full version which is when it fully (or so it claims) does what you want it to.

The little guy – Patronising expression for consumers. Never to be used for anyone who is vertically challenged.

Loop someone in / keep them in the loop – My mind wanders to Billy Crystal in the film 'City Slickers' learning to lasso cattle, with the person who says 'loop you in' wielding a rope headed for my neck. Forgive me if I don't listen further.

Loss leaders – A part of a business which is known to lose money but deemed acceptable for the other benefits it brings. Lost leaders are known to lose money but deemed acceptable for the other benefits it is hoped they might bring. I have also met a number of leading losers but that's another story.

M

Marathon not a sprint – Similar to 'I'm playing the long game'. For this read, 'I was a bit slow to get started'.

Mast – As in 'pin or nail your colours to the mast'. To set out your beliefs and opinions. Believed to derive from the colours (or flags) which hang from a ship's mast. See also put a stake in the ground. Used because the game of pin the tail on the donkey is socially awkward.

Mechanisms – Methods. We use coping mechanisms as advised by counsellors and life coaches, or should I call them career mechanics?

Meet with – Increasingly this is being used rather than simply 'meet'. A financial journalist told me this was one of his pet peeves: "Meet will do most of the time, the word implies you're coming into contact with someone. It is pretty critical part of its definition."

Metabolic rate, upping the – This is a recent addition – 'we need to up the metabolic rate of a project'. Do they mean raise the heart rate? Doesn't it just mean speed something up?

Mindmapping – A method used to capture and set out ideas which are linked to a central concept – it is less about mapping my mind, more using my mind to create a map.

Mindsets – A way of thinking. Also sounds like headsets – where's your headset? For a moment I thought I was on a long haul flight and about to miss the film.

Mindsharing – Sharing ideas. Another very silly expression – why would you share a mind?

Put it in your mindwok and stir it – Seriously chop everything in to small pieces and flash fry them?! Although perhaps I judge too quickly. I have been in plenty of meetings where I've left with my brain feeling sufficiently stir-fried.

GLOSSARY OF EXPRESSIONS

De minimis – A fund management editor best explains this: "By a mile, is the most f*cking annoying term at present, when people just mean minimal or minor. Presumably users think Latin makes them sound important. Grrr." Q.E.D.

Mission critical – A pivotal part of a project which, if not successful, can undermine and unbalance a project. Mission critical is a ridiculous use of two words. You're not Tom Cruise. Important would do just as well.

Mission statement – A statement which explains the purpose and objective of the business. Does make we wonder what would be the mission statement of mission control? The secret of a good mission statement is brevity – an omission statement?

Money shot – The thing which will earn the cash. Increasingly people talk in business talk about idea being a money shot even when there are no cameras. Apparently originates from pornography. I can think of some people who think they could be porn stars, bless.

Monetise (our relationships) – To find a way to make some money from something – also used as commercialise ... I like to think also of profitise, cashise, retirise (these don't exist, but if the logic follows, ought to). "Monetise sounds just a bit too mercenary" – and that was from a stockbroker salesman, or as I call him 'an honest broker'.

Mousetrap, build a better – This expression is a derivation of the quote from 19th century American poet, Ralph Waldo Emerson. It means to develop or invent a product which is better than one which exists today. Emerson said, "Build a better mousetrap, the world will beat a path to your door." Can we make it a humanitarian one? (There's a reason why they're humanitarian not mousitarian; more about me than the mouse.)

My bad – I hate this one. Please, please don't use it. It is my mistake.

N

Navel gazing – To spend one's time thinking about ourselves, presumably our core competencies. Not a nautical expression, a reference to one's belly button.

Needle (move the) – To have made progress – ooh, demonstrable progress, you needle-mover, you. Nothing to do with sewing or vinyl records (Some may have to look this up, sadly. Hint: precursor to CDs – it's what people used to get their Val Doonican fix).

Network – To meet and talk people into handing over a business card. Attrition, basically. Also used in computing.

NFN – Normal for Norfolk. Normal for Norfolk was created by doctors at the Norfolk and Norwich Hospital to categorise some of their more 'intellectually challenged' patients. According to the 'Literary Norfolk' website, these patients were usually from Dereham. The term was then abbreviated to NFN. which could easily be added to case notes for the purposes of quick reference.

Nines – As in 'dressed to the nines'. It was believed that the best suits used nine yards of cloth (see also whole nine yards); if someone is impeccably dressed or dressed up for an occasion they are 'dressed to the nines'. I tend to come in at about 5.75.

Note to self – I use this a lot. Note to self in writing a book about corporate idioms – I will never be able to use one again without expecting to be pulled up for it.

No-brainer – Straightforward decisions which require little consideration. It just doesn't sit right with me. If you can't stomach something you wouldn't say it's a no-stomacher. If you can't handle something it isn't a no-handler.

Noodle – 'Getting your noodle around something' – giving something some thought. Few know where it comes from – one thought is from a noddle, in turn derived from nod. Hmm, maybe.

O

Obviously – This is guaranteed to make me very cross. What may be obvious to you likely isn't to me. If it was obvious you wouldn't need to explain it to me. You are also suggesting that I am a total fool for not knowing because it is, after all, entirely obvious. I don't obviously think that people use it on purpose. Obviously, I think that people just sprinkle sentences with it, just like they use other words, like like, obviously.

Octane – As in high octane – reference to high performance engineering with connotations of businesses working like finely-tuned machinery. Now, where did I put the keys?

Officing from home – To work at home. Ridiculous. You wouldn't reverse this by talking about doing personal errands at work (e.g. online food shopping, planning the weekend, taking personal calls) as homing from office – makes you sound like a pigeon.

Offline – As in 'taking it offline'. To not discuss something in the current setting, but wait until we have left the room or hung up on the conference call. "I didn't know we were ever online and thank goodness you added the word 'line' – I had a horrible feeling you were going to strip."

Offsite – A meeting which takes place in a room with a flip chart, but is made all the more exotic and exciting because it is not on your usual premises. Not to be confused with an oversight (which I am now calling an übersight), which is the topic ignored by the agenda, also known as the elephant in the room.

On board – Onboarding clients means getting them set up. Also used as in 'taking an idea on board' which means I'm going to pretend that I have heard you, but haven't. In fact I have dismissed your idea even before you finished your sentence. See also I hear you. Getting on board means being in agreement with an idea or approach.

Onion (peel the) – To remove a few layers or pull an idea apart. Makes me cry every time.

Operationalising – to do something. I have heard this in the context of 'operationalising the strategy' or shouldn't we essentially talk about tacticulating the strategy? In which case click open a box of small mints and think outside the tictactics as you tictacticulate.

Opportunities – Challenges vs problems – a positive spin on a bad, bad situation, and it's getting more and more absurd.

Orders of magnitude – Much. The business was an order of magnitude larger. Just say much larger.

Organic growth – Growth without requiring a transaction or injection of financing. Like fruit and vegetables, firms with organic growth are similar to others but with imperfections, such as a dirty mark-up.

Outage – A newswire journalist raised this as annoying expression used "instead of a power or system failure".

Outside the box – To think imaginatively and laterally. Why don't we say outside the cube, or is that too multi-dimensional?

Outturn – Often used as a financial result. A national journalist told me "No, it's either revenue or profits, the rest is deliberate obfuscation."

Taking ownership – Taking responsibility and probably the blame. All aboard the good ship ownership.

GLOSSARY OF EXPRESSIONS

P

Package – Let's package that idea and monetise it – i.e. brand it, give it a bit of a marketing push and sell it.

Page, on the same – To agree with each other. Neither of us are sheets of paper or parts of a book. See singing from same hymn sheet.

Pain points – Irritations like price points. Makes me think of an after-dinner port headache. You can put your finger on it.

Paradigm shift – A significant change. Hello, would you like a paradigm shifting solution? Not really, I don't know what that means. See also game changer.

Park an idea – To leave it aside for a moment while discussion focuses elsewhere. "It is an idea, not a car" said one freelance pensions journalist. Literally, this is the act of 'popping it on a post-it and we'll come back to it later', which as a head of trading of a global brokerage firm pointed out, is an expression in its own right. See also backburner.

Parts, lots of moving – Many elements to a project. What surprises me is the surprise with which people declare 'well, this project has lots of moving parts'. All projects have lots of moving parts.

Square peg, round hole – The general idea is that it's a misfit, but this isn't exactly the case …. If it's a large square hole and relatively smaller round peg, what's the problem?

Pear shaped – As in 'it's all gone a bit pear shaped'. Gone a bit wrong. Also used as a female body shape. I have always said that the good Lord above looks down on me and says "Oh she went a bit pear shaped". See also Pete Tong.

Penetration – There are too many people talking about penetration. Used in the context of market share – what's our market penetration? Did you receive a full 'share' is, however, a perfectly feasible question when it comes to sexual satisfaction.

Performant – Does what it should and well. The price and proof points are proof positive that the product is performant.

Pete Tong – A modern twist on cockney rhyming slang for wrong: 'it's all gone a bit Pete Tong'. Pete Tong is/was a club DJ from the 1990s – apparently he was very good so this is not a reference to either Mr Tong or his abilities, he was just in the wrong (or right, bearing in mind he is now immortalised) rhyming place at the wrong (or right) time. Name of 2004 film about clubbing in Ibiza – I had to be told that because I am not Street innit (I am Streets).

Pickle, in a – To be in a difficult or awkward situation ... er, which some will relish? Sorry.

> **Pie.** Plenty of servings.
>
> **Pie in the sky** – An entirely unrealistic idea, one which is unlikely to be achieved – probably lots of the ideas in the blue sky thinking brainstorm.
>
> **Throw pies in the dark** – To take a haphazard approach. I do not condone food fights, never have, never will – and in the dark? Messy.
>
> **Easy as pie** – Something that is exceptionally straightforward and easy to achieve. Just don't be tempted to throw them, and if you are, I am guessing the lights are on.
>
> **Eat humble pie** – Admittance that one was incorrect and needs to apologise. Generally not thrown around easily.
>
> **Pie-eyed** – Completely drunk. Here's one in the eye – presumably a thrown pie?

Pig in treacle – Something which is slow and seems to struggle to perform as it should – for example, 'trading systems that run like a pig in treacle'.

GLOSSARY OF EXPRESSIONS

Pigeon – To try lots of things to see which one would work. As in 'had to send out a whole flock of pigeons to see which ones come back to roost'. I like the idea of throwing out a lot of pigeon pies (happily no longer listed on the pie menu), presumably in the dark.

Let's put a pin it – This has two meanings – either to burst an idea, or to be precise and specific. Opposite of throw in a grenade, when we pull the pin out.

Pitcher catcher strategy – As a country manager of an international poker company explained: "This is another annoying new one. 'We aim to implement a pitcher catcher strategy – pitch the idea, catch it and run. Yeah Baby!' Ugh." As a point of order it was pointed out to me that apparently you have to choose either to pitch, catch or run. I have no idea, but it sounds logical to me.

In the plan – Being taken into account. If someone in a meeting says 'it's in the plan' it usually means 'Oops, I forgot about that, but will do it straight after the meeting'.

Platform – Anything on which technology runs – trading platforms, software platforms, operating platforms. Whenever anyone gets some media coverage, we refer to them having a platform. A raised area on which a speaker stands. Something to jump off if you're at the leading edge.

Lot on my plate – Someone who is busy and is asserting they are busier than anyone else. If you have a lot on your plate, reduce your calorie intake or raise your metabolic rate.

Play, all to play for – when the stakes are high and every effort is put into achieving the goal. Throwing everything you possibly can at something to succeed.

Plum job – Well paid job considered easy to fulfil. Why plums I don't know – maybe they were low hanging fruit?

Plum in your mouth – Someone deemed to be upper class as judged by their accent. 'Speak with a plum in their mouth' – served on a silver spoon?

Plunge, take the – committing to taking action despite being anxious, cautious or concerned. Not to be confused with bath, taking an early.

Pocket, out of – Expenses born by an individual which requires form filling in order to be reimbursed. Usually machine-washed taxi receipts discovered stuffed in my pocket weeks after the expenses deadline.

Poisoned chalice – Taking on a project known by others to be destined to failure or to catch you out. You haven't learned the sleight of hand of switching goblets then – have medieval films taught you nothing?

Pond, across the – slang expression for across the Atlantic. It tends to be used by UK and US executives to describe each other's location.

Going postal – Workplace rage and extreme anger which cannot be controlled and which leads to an act of violence. Derives from a series of incidents when US postal service workers shot and killed colleagues, management and police officers. For a sense of what going postal feels like, take a Northern Line train at 8am any day, Monday to Friday.

Hot potato – Usually referred to in the context of dropping something like a hot potato. As soon as someone has got what they need, they stop associating with you or they pass the buck without taking much or any responsibility. Also used in terms of a topic deemed to be highly contentious.

Powerhouse – Aspect of strength in an organisation. Meant as a compliment, mostly considered to be quite patronising. See also glue, lifeblood and engine room.

GLOSSARY OF EXPRESSIONS

Pressing flesh – Meeting people, often used in political context to meet the public/fans – not to be confused with pinch an inch, a rough approximation of body fat, or in my case, grab a slab.

Price points – = Price. Derived from the supply and demand curve. Various points along the curve which determine or reflect the price of a product or service. Just say price.

Proof is in the pudding – You can have the best ingredients (although you still can't beat licking the bowl) but only when the pudding is made will the taste test determine how good it is and whether it is a performant pudding.

Proof points – Examples and marking points along the 'banker' curve.

Proof positive – Proof positive shows that I (or anyone else who has made the assertion) was correct. I used to use this a lot and rather liked it. Better than 'just goes to show', 'told you so' or 'nah, nah, ne nah, nah'.

Punch above your weight – Boxing reference to fighting someone in a heavier league than yourself. For clarity, I am not condoning contact sports in the workplace, but white collar boxers, knock yourself out.

Punt, take a – To have a go at something even if it isn't fully thought through and/or tested. To act on a feeling, just like the one where you thought you could navigate a flat-bottomed boat on the river in Cambridge.

Purpose – Is an individual, product or service fit for purpose – i.e. good for the use for which he/she/it was intended. What a concept. Also used as purpose and repurpose – let's purpose the collateral (a bit like put it to work, give it a purpose). Re-purpose, to take something (usually text) and re-use it in a slightly different form, i.e. to repackage.

Pursuing other interests – Fired. See also family, spending time with.

Pushing treacle up a hill – To be hard to achieve, and frankly why would you want to? Also used with water – pushing water.

Q

Quantum leap – Frequently used incorrectly – often used to mean a significant move, but as a former CIO of an investment management firm described it to me, "It is used to mean a 'major change' when it is the smallest possible step change". See also decimate. There is a TV programme of this name still doing the rounds on satellite TV.

Quarter – A three month period. Often expressed as a segment as 'this quarter'. We don't ever talk about 'this halfer'. In business, we live our lives in quarters, forever comparing QonQ.

Quarterback – Project manager/project leader – we think. The CEO of a financial markets consultancy said she had heard someone use this: "Quarterbacking. Who's going to quarterback this project – it's lingo for project manage, I think!"

Question – As in 'that's a good question' (in response to ANY quality of question). Right up there with the use of 'absolutely' when seconds later it is clear that the person disagrees.

R

Radar – As in 'on my radar'. I am aware of it. Under the radar means I got away with it. You can't beat the military for making us feel more important in our glass and steel meeting rooms.

Rationalisation – Best described by a freelance journalist: "Rationalisation – a term used to avoid saying 'sacking people'. Ironically, it means inventing an explanation after the event, to sustain the false impression that life is rational."

Reach out – To proactively communicate with someone. First place on the 'Lingua Franca Podium of Irritation.'

If you use it, chances are I will not hear what you say next. In my mind three soul singers are synchronised swaying and singing 'I'll be there, with a love that will see you through … when you feel like you can't go on … darling reach out, reach out." Evidently I am not alone in my frustration.

As the country manager of an international poker company put it, "I hate it when people say the following: 'if you have any questions, please feel free to reach out'."

My bond trader friend added, "When I'm asked by a New Yorker, I have to ask how long are his arms?"

"It is so ridiculous!", cried a London marketing manager. "I'm not 'reaching out', I'm asking the relevant department for information that falls within their remit to provide. I'm not asking them to help me with a personal problem, or for a donation to charity. I'm simply asking them to do what they're meant to do and frankly, I'm not prepared to beg! I find it amazing that people could just say it with a straight face as if it was a totally normal phrase – and as if they couldn't hear Diana Ross in their heads … 'Reach out and touch somebody's hand, make this world a better place if we can…'. Laughable really." And one of my team asked, "I just wonder what are they going to touch?"

GLOSSARY OF EXPRESSIONS

Read-out – Technically this is the process of removing information from an electronic/automated device and displaying in a readable form. One head of financial services, EMEA for an IT infrastructure firm told me this is used in the form of "'We are going to have a read-out'. This can be insulting to the presenter, implying he or she is just reading the text on the slides and it's one-way communication".

Real time – At the moment in question – real time, as opposed to fake time or mythical time.

Reality is – when what you mean to say is 'in reality' – Reality is we need to do this. Actually, we need to do this. Let's make it a reality and actually stop it.

Red herring – Something which is introduced to deliberately confuse the matter or throw someone onto a different direction. Red herrings are salted herrings which I believe turn red during the smoking process. Also alludes to throwing people 'off a scent' from using herrings to lay false trails to confuse hunting dogs.

Redundancy – In information technology, the term redundant has several usages. Computer or network system components are installed to provide system back-up in case primary resources fail. It also means unnecessary or duplicated information, or extra binary digits generated to ensure that no bits are lost during the transference of data. Of course it does. In human terms it means no longer being required and therefore you can spend more time with your family – most likely because you will have been replaced by a computer. See also downsizing and rightsizing.

Relationship management – Customer relationship management. A system for monitoring your sales force monitoring their customers, who are monitoring your product or service.

Respect – As in 'with all due respect'. As a publisher put it to me, it means "I very condescendingly disagree with you."

Retroactive – Refers to a back-dated pay rise or acting on something which happened in the past. A retrosexual is someone who looks pretty sexy by wearing out of date fashions which weren't sexy back then either.

Revert – Come back to you. Often used as a sign-off at the end of an email. 'Will revert. Rgds J.'

Rightsizing – See downsizing and redundancy.

Between a rock and a hard place – To be caught in between two difficult circumstances or choices. Some believe this refers to a financial crisis which particularly affected the railroad and mining industries of the Western states of the US. In 1917, the Arizona copper mines' labour unions confronted the management with a list of demands which they were denied, and many workers were forcibly deported to New Mexico. As such, they faced a choice between terrible conditions working the rocks in Arizona or the prospect of unemployment and poverty in New Mexico.

It's not rocket science – No, it's not so why point it out? One of my clients told me a story about a friend of his, a fellow engineer, who was in a meeting with a too-clever-for-his-own-good sales person who led the discussion with the statement: 'Well, you do not need to be a rocket scientist...' At that point, the prospect on the other side of the table interrupted to introduce their colleague: 'This is Dr XYZ, formerly of NASA, and we hired him because he is a rocket scientist'. The conversation was then handed over to the engineer and the scientist, leaving the sales person rather floundering in the background.

Rocket, send it up in a – To test an idea. I know what I'd like to send up in a rocket – it's not rocket science.

Rope, money for old – When a customer pays for a product which is out of date and probably not entirely effective for its intended use. Also used when 'looping in' (see in the loop) and when flogging a dead horse, so why waste good rope on it? The question is, how long is a piece of old rope?

Rubber, when the rubber hits the road – to launch something, take it out of testing conditions and see if it works or gets a puncture.

Rubber, burn some – To get started as quickly as possible. From sudden acceleration of a car from a standing position. Note: rubber is also another word for a condom or an eraser, so best to be specific. When trying to motivate a team, a battle cry of 'let's burn some condom' might not get the results you were seeking.

S

Salt, take it with a pinch of – Don't take it seriously. If you add a pinch of salt it is supposed to make it easier to swallow, but don't overdo it 5-6g a day is the recommend daily average.

Salt, worth your – To do your job well, to be worth your salary but don't exceed your daily average.

Scale – Scale, up scale, down scale, right scale, wrong scale, under scale, über scale it's gone off the scale.

Grand scheme/schematics – 'In the grand scheme of things' – in the context of the overall project, activity or situation. A schematic diagram uses graphics and abstract images to help explain a complex concept. Most schematics are pretty grand.

Secret sauce – The secret ingredient. As a freelance journalist said, "I also HATE the phrase 'secret sauce'. Bleurgh. It sounds like what you don't want on your kebab. Food ingredients should never be secret, it's actually illegal AND unhygienic."

(Up)selling – To get more business from existing customers, particularly by moving further up the organisation. Must be handled delicately otherwise it can be upsetting.

Sets – Toolset / mindset / headsets / get set / jet set / offset / upset. We love our sets.

Shoestring – To do a project with a much, much smaller (read ridiculously small) budget.

All over the shop – To be in a chaotic state. Why shop versus office I have no idea, but I have been in plenty of those too.

Talking shop – Talking about work outside the workplace. A talking shop is a forum for debate, but not necessarily decisions. Can also be known as most meetings.

Shoring – Onshoring / offshoring / overshoring / übershoring / upshoring / downshoring / areyoushoring – like outsourcing,

GLOSSARY OF EXPRESSIONS

insourcing, rightsourcing – we make a decision, then change it again, and again.

Shot in the arm – Something which gives a project or person renewed vigour. See Injection.

Show stoppers – Supposed to be something which is so amazing it pauses a theatrical production for the resounding applause. Often misused as something which is likely to cause a project to be cancelled and is used widely in technology projects – not that I think many of them will naturally be into musicals – unless it was the Big Bang Theory the Musical – that would be interesting. That said, I don't think you can beat office opera for fun. See singing from the same hymn sheet.

Sidecar to your question – The additional question which may require a helmet and driving gloves.

Singing from the same hymn sheet – Everyone doing the same thing. In quieter work moments, I've always enjoyed a bit of office opera – it's good for the soul, especially when used in normal/mundane moments like 'would you like a cup of tea' or more dramatic moments like 'oh no, woe is me, my stapler, my stapler oh oh oh my stapler has run out … of … staples.' And then, if colleagues are really singing from the same hymn sheet they chime in with [them:] 'poor you' [you:] 'woe is me' [them:] 'poor you'; 'woe is me' [you get the point], and then a colleague (ideally soprano, but not compulsory) pipes up, 'but wait! I have an idea!' 'An idea, an idea, she has an idea' 'yes an idea' 'an idea, an idea, she has an idea [avoid the temptation to overplay this – three times maximum, 10 can get tedious. What am I saying! Four is tedious, three is more than enough] … [cue soprano:] 'borrow mine!'.

An alternative if you do feel that a hymn sheet is actually necessary, why not sing company-wide emails: 'left to spend time with his family', 'valuable contribution', 'will be missed'… pause for four beats … 'So very pleased to announce the appointment of his successor ... highly experienced ... valuable contribution ....'

Skin in the game – To have a vested interest in something, usually financial. You scratch my face, I'll scratch yours. Allegedly, first used by the famous investor Warren Buffett to describe a situation where high ranking professionals in an organisation own a stake.

Slam dunk – An undisputed win or clear victory. Nothing to do with dunking biscuits in tea.

Sledgehammer to crack a nut – An excessive response to a situation.

Socialise the idea – To see what other people think / test the concept/idea on others. Unless you're talking about a social event such as team drinks, business and social should not be mixed over a glass of tepid chardonnay.

Socialise your brand – Test your brand. What's the opposite – hermitise the brand?

Solution – A product or service. We seem to love a good solution, particularly paradigm shifting solutions.

Soup to nuts – I have never understood this and like 'bump on a log' this has completely justified the book for me. Not only has it been a cathartic opportunity for me to vent my frustration, but also to justifiably admit my ignorance about the origin and meaning of some expressions. Soup to nuts is one of the expressions where I have wanted to stop a business discussion dead and cry, 'What on earth are you talking about?!'

'Soup to nuts' means from beginning to end. The alpha and omega of a situation. It is derived from a typical Roman meal where a meal would start with soup and end with nuts.

Sourcing – Outsourcing (when you have decided to give an element of a project to someone outside the organisation to do it); insourcing (when you realise that this wasn't the best

GLOSSARY OF EXPRESSIONS

approach); and rightsourcing (when you've done a combination of in and out – should also be called hokey cokey sourcing (a dance where participants bring their project in, source their project out, in out, in out and shake it all about).

Put a stake in the ground – To set out a position, view or stance on something. Not to be confused with putting a steak in the ground, because the big dogs will dig it up. I did wonder whether it had anything to do with being prepared to be burned at the stake for a belief. See also pin your colours to the mast.

Burned at the stake – Punished for something you believe in, possibly by your stakeholders. Burning at the stake in public was used a long time ago in England & Wales as a punishment for treason or witchcraft.

Stakeholders – Anyone who has an interest, vested or not, welcome or not. How do you like your stakeholder? Rare.

Standpoint – Point of view – after a while, what's the point of standing?

In step – To be marching in step with something is to agree with it, go along with it – not to be confused with insole, which is a cushion placed in a shoe to make the marching more comfortable – not very military.

Step change – Significant move. See quantum leap.

Perfect storm – When a rare set of circumstances combine to aggravate a situation. According to a UK publisher, "When there's more than one cause to an outcome, suddenly it's a perfect bloody storm. Annoying through over-use. Note, when one's own parents start using city jargon it really is time to stop using it."

Straw man – A concept where a product or service can be created in less than full detail (i.e a prototype), or where less than the full information is known and tested to find ways in which the final version can be improved. A first draft specifically designed for criticism and testing to wheedle out ideas which easily go up in flames.

Street – Cool. Down with the kids 'cos it's sick and phat. I recommend total avoidance.

String – How long is a piece of string? The usual response for 'what will it cost' or 'how long will it take'. Describes how hard it is to be specific when there are many variable elements involved.

Success – As in 'what does success look like?'. This is used a lot – for me, lying on a sunbed by a pool, cocktail in hand.

Suck it and see – This should never, ever be used. It is meant to give something a try, but the connotations are so grim it should be banned immediately. I think like sweet spot it is one of those expressions which people throw in to see whether you will giggle, flinch or raise an eyebrow and measure your level of maturity or whether you are completely asexual.

Sustainability – The longevity of something. The editor of a global magazine told me: "'Sustainability' is my bête noir right now, as is the use of 'national measures'(urgh! Kilos? Pounds? Bushels?) One of the worst press releases I have read was caked with jargon about 'national measures' and 'first generation sustainability reporting'."

SWAT team – A SWAT team is a group of law enforcement professionals trained to deal with highly dangerous or violent situations. No corporate situation could ever justify calling a group of people a SWAT team.

Swim lane – According to Forbes, this is a "specific responsibility within a business organization" … a dedicated area of a pool set aside for people to go up and down, up and down, up and … the question is: fast or slow?

Swimming against the tide – Working against a stronger force. For charity? Does it come with a sponsorship form?

GLOSSARY OF EXPRESSIONS

Live by the sword – If you fight, you must expect to be killed. Cheery.

The pen is mightier than the sword – Best not to irritate a journalist. PR people, take note.

Synergy/synergetic – Areas of overlap – not to be confused with energy/energetic. Most mergers and acquisitions (also called M&A, not to be confused with M&S and certainly not to be confused with S&M. But as I tell my mother, S&M is similar to M&S – they both have their own range of pants.) M&A is designed to create synergies, but before too long people lose the energy to create the synergy.

T

(Key) Take aways – The main things we have learned. My key take away is a curry, every time.

Take one for the team – To do something for the benefit of others, not yourself – what a concept! You 'one for the team taker, you'.

Team work makes for dream work – Just stop, now.

Coming under the tent – To invite someone into a privileged position, usually to learn information that most won't learn. Ah, the great British summer under canvas – it's fine, I'll stay indoors, even if it means I need to know less.

Tether our thinking – Presumably means to consolidate our thoughts. A head of communication in London put it, "I did hear someone say 'we need to tether our thinking', which I always assumed they made up. And I assume it meant 'agree' but I didn't ask. Actually, I might perpetuate that and see if it sticks …"

Thought leader – A visionary. A national columnist asked, "What the hell is a thought leader?" A US journalist agreed: "If I hear the term 'thought leadership' one more time, I cannot answer for the consequences. … What exactly do PR people think thought leadership is? Are they the supreme leaders who can dictate what people think? Or do they actually believe that no one else in financial tech has ever had the same thought?"

(Let me) think on that – What we mean to say is let me think about that. Shorthand for "I've made a decision but I'll pretend to consider your ideas." We don't think on things. We think about things. Roundabouts don't become roundons. At the next roundon please turn right. Let's hope he doesn't get a hardabout.

Throw your toys out of the pram – Need I say more? We have all been in these types of meetings. I have even sat on the naughty step.

GLOSSARY OF EXPRESSIONS

Tiger team – According to Forbes: "A 'tiger team' is a group of experts – specifically a bunch of tech geeks entrusted with curing your computer ills." Grrr.

Tits up / belly up – When something has gone wrong. Derived from animals dying on their backs. Be careful about where to use 'tits up'– not everyone likes it. If a project is 'going south' cosmetic surgery may help. See also pear shaped, Pete Tong and balls up.

Top down approach – To look at something from the highest level downwards – but if you're ever asked, don't take your top down. The opposite of bottom up approach.

Touching base – Let's catch up. Derives from baseball – touching the base as you pass it. Used extensively in business. Let's touch base? Well, you're not touching mine. The worst thing I heard is that a chain of hotels calls its business centres 'touchbase centres'. You see now I want one, I want a touchbase centre – not an office or a meeting room or a watercooler, I want a touchbase centre. Mine's called the kettle.

Touchpaper – As in, light the blue touchpaper and stand back. To say something controversial. Why is it called touchpaper when you shouldn't touch it? Throw in a grenade.

Traction, gaining – I have to say I do use this a lot. As a campaign begins to make an impact and build momentum, I do say that it gains traction. Can't help but think of very big (spare) tyres every time I use it, though.

U

U-shaped – This was used to describe a curve, but now describes a general trend where events were progressing well, then dropped off dramatically and in a short space of time, remained steady at a lower level before picking up dramatically in a short space of time again. For me it takes me back to my geography lessons (u-shaped valleys).

über – amazing, incredible .... that's so like über cool. Derived from German for above.

Unique – 'We are almost unique in that respect …' which was the ranked the most irritating by a London financial and business journalist. Really, how could you possibly, truly know?

Upcycling – This is a newish one. As a member of my team told me, "It is used when people say you can make more money out of waste than the original product made."

Upstream – As in 'we're moving upstream'. To move higher up a business or chain of command. 'Our goal is to move upstream'… is that with or without a paddle?

User experience – Customer test or customer usage. Anything with the word 'experience' in it drives me crazy. 'Ultimate user experience' sends me up the wall.

Utilise – We use things, we don't utilise them. Words – utilise them, don't abutilise them. Unusual should then become unutilisual, surely. Bloody utiliseless.

V

Value add – Also known as added value. 'What's the 'value add?' … we use adding value or value add to the point of gagging, you could say ad*d* nauseam.

Value chain – value at every point of a process. Used right along the value chain. We add value at every point of the value chain. But doesn't every chain have its points of weakness?

Corporate values – To be honest and kind and to be good and faithful. Think of it as a firm's wedding vow to you and its customers, apart from the 'till death do us part' bit.

Verticals – Units and segments of an industry. I'm in the financial vertical and the wine and spirits horizontal.

Vis-à-vis – In relation or in respect of something. This drove me mad in the 90s. This was a classic example of an expression we believed made us sound more intelligent. Occasionally I would chip in: 'voulez-vous vis-a-vis visa visage'. Meaningless, but irresistible.

W

Walk the walk – To take action rather than simply talk about it; to illustrate that you actually know what you're talking about. Often used in conjunction with talk the talk – if you're going to talk the talk, you have got to walk the walk – oh, just shut up and get on with it.

Ware – Stuff, basically. Hardware, software … Next time you need to call the IT helpdesk, casually say 'It may be a softstuff issue, than a hardstuff one'; and then (don't ask me why it just seems a natural progression), call them hotstuff (before receiving your P45 and packing your desk). Ignore me.

> **Water.** It's everywhere.
>
> **Hold water** –To stand up to examination. If an argument or an explanation of something is not robust enough to prove correct under examination and can be disproved, destabilised or shown to be unfounded, it is deemed that it does not hold water.
>
> **Make your mouth water** –Temptation. Activation of the salivation glands because something smells good. The temptation to gossip by the water cooler is enough to make your mouth water.
>
> **Test the water/waters** – To test something out before becoming fully committed. A bit like trying out the local swimming pool before signing up for a membership; also referred to as dipping a toe in the water, which is how a friend of mine tends to get in when we go swimming, an inch at a time until she is finally submerged, at which point it is time to leave.
>
> **Treading water** – Despite effort, one's situation remains stationary – and that is stationary with an a, not an e as in office supplies and writing materials. Otherwise despite effort, one's situation remains enveloped, whether pushed or not.

GLOSSARY OF EXPRESSIONS

Walk on water – To possess super-heroic qualities. Derived from the biblical reference to Jesus walking on water. The less said the better.

Watermark, or high water mark – Used in terms of investment as the highest peak of value that an investment fund or an account has achieved. Derived from the highest level that a sea or river has reached at a particular place.

It is what it is – You don't say.

Wheel, reinventing the – The most fundamental of inventions. Nothing can improve on it other than being able to twitch one's nose, like Samatha in the TV – later film – 'Bewitched' as a mode of transport after a late night out. In some parts of England they try piles of bricks as a wheel replacement, but with limited success and maximum annoyance.

Wholesale – This tends to be used in the context of 'I'll tell you everything', which is incorrect usage. 'I'll quote you this wholesale, share this with you wholesale'. Wholesale is when something is purchased with a view to reselling for business use, versus retail when it is purchased for private use. Wholesale can turn into retail if I were buying chocolate to sell on, some of it may not make it to market.

Wild card – Where a participant who usually wouldn't get a chance to participate is given a chance. From card games, particularly poker – playing the joker or a card which can have any value.

Window of opportunity – A short period of time in which something should be done, before the window gets closed again. If you use this expression I will have doubleglazed over.

Windows – Used in diarising and calendarising terms (or should it be 'Outlookising'?). A timeslot – often used as 'I have a 'window.' By the same token, I have a window ledge. The moment just before a meeting with someone who has a window, I want to jump off it.

Win-win scenario – Everyone's a winner – no-one loses. I believe it is rarely a matter of win-win. It is always a comparative outcome – one party will always do better than the other party. Life's just not like that. See also wading through treacle, pushing water uphill, swimming against the tide. It's called a day in the life in the office.

Workshop it – Let's think about it. A CEO of financial markets consultancy pointed out, "workshop seems to have become a verb". Let's flipchart it and see what tears off?

World class – What is world class really? Who knows? World beating was the worst reference I have ever seen. Really? Is your leading product really world beating? If world class, why not globe class?

Worst case scenarios – Planning for the worst possible eventuality. I love worst case scenario planning – plan well and you should never be disappointed. A pessimist's delight.

X, Y

Yard arm – As in 'the sun is over the yard arm'. In the North Atlantic, the sun would rise over the upper mast at around 11am. This would coincide with the instruction to 'stand easy' at forenoon when officers would go below for their first rum shot of the day. The expression reflects the ideal time to have a first alcoholic drink for the day, but not to be encouraged unless on holiday with a cocktail by the beach. Please drink responsibly.

Yardstick – A definitive measure of something. It derives from a measuring tool which sets out exactly the length of a yard.

Z

Zeitgeist – To capture the mood, the spirit of the times. Judging from the emails I received in response to my survey, we are overusing corporate expressions, as you may have realised.

Zero sum game – A situation where gain by one party is exactly offset by a corresponding loss by another party, therefore balancing out the result. Wikipedia uses an analogy I particularly like, with regard to cake. When cutting a cake, where taking a larger piece reduces the amount of cake available for others, is a zero sum game if all participants value each unit of cake equally. Quite, except for the fact that I will likely value the cake more highly than most.

APPENDIX – A SELECTION OF BASEBALL EXPRESSIONS

Ballparks – In the right ballpark (broadly in the right area), ballpark figures (estimates) and out of the ballpark (something done either exactly as it should be, or particularly well). Ballparks is derived from baseball.

Big league(s) – At the highest professional level. Used to describe higher echelons of business and commerce.

Brand new ball game; whole other ball game – A dramatic turn of events or signifying something completely unrelated, different, or irrelevant.

To throw a bean ball – A ball intentionally thrown at a batter's head. In politics, it can be a verbal assault or a policy that is targeted to seriously hurt a particular opponent or group.

Bush league – Amateur league, implying a lack of professionalism and unsophistication.

Cleanup hitter – The fourth person in batting order, who is expected to hit it hard so that the previous players who may be waiting at the bases can also 'run home' to score runs. In business, someone who comes in to solve a problem or lead a team.

Closer – A closing pitcher brought in to finish the game. In business, the person brought in to close the deal, get things done

Cover your bases – A fielding player 'covers a base' by standing close to prevent the opposing running player from reaching it safely. In business, it is used to explain being ready for every possible outcome.

Curve ball – A pitch which is delivered to surprise and confound the batter by curving unexpectedly. In business, an unexpected event, often from left-field.

Double header – Two competitive events with the same contestants on a single day.

Down to the last out – Also known as 'down to the last strike' – to be near the end of the contest. To have just one last chance, to be near the end of the competition.

Extra Innings – an extension of the time allocated to settle an issue or break a tie.

First base – A batter may hope to reach first base and then continue around second and third bases until he reaches 'home'. In romantic relations, a kiss is referred to as the first base.

Grand slam – Any sudden sweeping victory. A batter who hits a home run with bases loaded has hit a four-run 'grand slam', a term originally borrowed from contract bridge for winning thirteen tricks. The term also can refer to anything good which comes in four parts, such as a 'grand slam breakfast'. It was a total fry up?

Grandstanding – A player attempting to win the support of fans in the grandstand by playing up to them is said to be grandstanding. In other contexts playing to the crowd, the media or any audience might be considered grandstanding. Happens all the time, I thank you.

Ground ball – A ball which when batted bounces or rolls along the ground. An achievement deemed to be underwhelming.

Hardball (playing hardball) – Comparison between the hardness of balls in baseball and softball. Business professionals when playing aggressively are called playing hardball. Not a sexual reference.

Heavy hitter – A player who gets a lot of home runs by hitting the ball very hard – also known as a slugger. Suggests may not be highly sophisticated or strategic but gets results by 'slugging' it out. (Also called a slogger in English, but not a baseball term.)

Home run – When a batter hits the ball with sufficient force that it ends up outside the playing field or stadium. In business referred to as a complete success (opposite of strike out, which is a failure).

Knock the cover off the ball – To exceed expectation. Hitting the ball so hard the leather covering comes off. In the early days of baseball a single ball was used for the whole game and the leather used to wear thin and exceptionally hard hitters would succeed in knocking the cover off.

Left of field – Unanticipated. History appears divided on its origin. Some say it refers to Babe Ruth who was a right fielder and a left-handed hitter. His fans bought tickets for the left side of the field, but Ruth's home runs mostly were hit out to the right field. Another refers to The University of Illinois College of Medicine where the Neuropsychiatric Institute building was located on the former left field home of Chicago Cubs in West Side Park. Led to suggestion that left field also refers to irrational.

Ninth inning – Suggestion that an event or process is near the end, that is in the last of a nine-inning game. Sometimes also used an alternative to a 'swansong'.

Off base – To be taken by surprise. Referring to a runner being away from a base and being caught or stumped out.

One base at a time – A strategy of moving players along one base at a time rather than adopting powerful hitting and high scoring. Also suggests a step by step approach. Also referred to as hitting singles or playing small ball.

Play ball – Called out by the umpire to start or restart the game. Also means to cooperate.

Rain check – An outdoor event spectator is given a ticket which either entitles them to refund or admission at a later date should it be interrupted by rain. It is an assurance of an offer to be taken up at a later date.

Relief pitcher – The replacement for another pitcher – acts as a substitute for the initial or regular occupant of a job.

Right off the bat – Immediately; without any delay.

Screwball – A pitch intended to behave erratically by being given a spin. Also refers to eccentric behaviour.

Softball questions – To ask easy questions. Deemed to be opposite of playing hardball (i.e. baseball) when difficult questions are fired at the respondent.

Stepping up to the plate – a batter's approach to the batting plate – used to express that someone has to 'step up' to a challenge.

Strike – Used in variety of ways including 'strike out', 'three strikes, you're out', 'a strike against you', 'he was born with two strikes against him'. In baseball, a strike is when the batter swings at and misses a pitch, or when the pitch crosses the strike zone without the batter swinging. A batter with three strikes is out and must stop batting.

Switch-hitter – Ambidextrous player (capable of hitting as a left-handed or right-handed batter). More broadly, 'switch-hitting' can refer to an ability to perform double functions or roles.

Taking cuts –Refers to a batter swinging the bat, sometimes said to 'take cuts' at the ball. Someone 'taking cuts' at somebody else is taking a verbal swing or attempting to strike a blow at another's reputation.

Endnote: Please do get in touch

CONGRATULATIONS for making it through. Letting this book go to print was a very hard decision. Even as I write these closing lines, I am receiving emails with new expressions. A lawyer wrote that she had been in a meeting where someone had told her they should 'get pregnant with the deal'. An editor of a trading publication asked why we say 'net, net', rather than simply 'net' and he'd even heard someone say 'net, net, net'.

I would love to hear from you. Searching Finance has set up a facebook page called The Lingua Franca of the Corporate Banker. I would be delighted if you would 'like' it or do get in touch by email:

Julia@streetsinthecity.com.

I hope that you enjoyed the book and thank you for reading, flicking and/or giving it.

Julia

www.ingramcontent.com/pod-product-compliance
Ingram Content Group UK Ltd.
Pitfield, Milton Keynes, MK11 3LW, UK
UKHW021325180426
11947UKWH00017B/1442

9 781907 720581